Donated by Lady Morse for 'Blooming Manipur'.

CALAMITY AND COURAGE

Other books by Belinda Morse

John Hanson Walker: the life and times of a Victorian Artist (Alan Sutton 1987)
Square Mile Walks (Historical Publications 1989)
A Woman of Design, A Man of Passion: the pioneering McIans (The Book Guild 2001)

CALAMITY AND COURAGE

A Heroine of the Raj

Belinda Morse

Book Guild Publishing
Sussex, England

First published in Great Britain in 2008 by
The Book Guild Ltd
Pavilion View
19 New Road
Brighton, BN1 1UF

Copyright © Belinda Morse 2008

The right of Belinda Morse to be identified as the author of this work has been asserted by her in accordance with the Copyright, Designs and Patents Act 1988.

All rights reserved. No part of this publication may be reproduced, transmitted, or stored in a retrieval system, in any form or by any means, without permission in writing from the publisher, nor be otherwise circulated in any form of binding or cover other than that in which it is published and without a similar condition being imposed on the subsequent purchaser.

Typesetting in Times by
YHT Ltd, London

Printed in Great Britain by
CPI Antony Rowe

A catalogue record for this book is available from
The British Library.

ISBN 978 1 84624 215 1

*Dedicated to the people of Manipur,
in the hope that peace may return to
their beautiful country.*

Belinda Morse, 27 March 2008

Contents

List of Illustrations		ix
Foreword		xv
1	A Posting to Manipur	1
2	A Palace Coup	15
3	Under Fire	28
4	A Torturous Escape	41
5	Headline News	50
6	A National Heroine	65
7	Ethel and the Queen	80
8	Publication of *My Three Years in Manipur*	93
9	A New World	103
10	In Ethel's Footsteps	115
Bibliography		131
Index		133

List of Illustrations

1. Map of Manipur drawn from a British Library military map of 1891 — xviii
2. A Naga house in Manipur *(Illustrated London News Picture Library)* — 4
3. Old suspension bridge in N. E. India *(The Alkazi Collection of Photography)* — 7
4. Head of a Naga chief on the border of Manipur *(Illustrated London News Picture Library)* — 8
5. Hillside village in N. E. India in the 1870s *(The Alkazi Collection of Photography)* — 9
6. Manipuri polo players, 1891 *(Illustrated London News Picture Library)* — 12
7. Maharajah Kulachandra *(By kind permission of The Maharaj Kumari Binodini Collection)* — 19
8. The British Residency at Manipur defended by the Gurkhas *(Illustrated London News Picture Library)* — 26
9. Plan of the fort and royal palace and their surroundings, 1891 adapted from R.E. Survey of 1891 — 32
10. The palace gates through which Commissioner Quinton and his party vanished *(Illustrated London News Picture Library)* — 37
11. Fugitives from the Manipur Residency fighting on the road *(Illustrated London News Picture Library)* — 45

12. Ethel St. Clair Grimwood *(Illustrated London News Picture Library)*   53

13. Frank Grimwood, Political Agent at Manipur *(Illustrated London News Picture Library)*   54

14. Lieutenant Grant wounded at the battle of Khongjom carried back to Tammu *(Illustrated London News Picture Library)*   59

15. The palace enclosure at Manipur: scene of Frank Grimwood's murder *(Illustrated London News Picture Library)*   62

16. Lieutenant Walter Simpson *(Illustrated London News Picture Library)*   64

17. The Thangal General, Regent and Senapati after their capture *(Illustrated London News Picture Library)*   78

18. Ethel photographed after being decorated by the Queen with the Royal Red Cross *(Hulton Archive, Getty Images Gallery)*   82

19. The young Maharajah Churachand *(By kind permission of The Maharaj Kumari Binodini Collection)*   91

20. Ethel's photograph by Vandyk taken from the frontispiece of *My Three Years in Manipur (author)*   95

21. Ethel's portrait by John Hanson Walker *(author)*   104

Colour plates (between pages 110 and 111)

The Women's Market, Imphal *(author)*

Bean seller in the Women's Market *(author)*

The Manipur polo team *(author)*

The walls surrounding the old royal palace, Manipur *(author)*

Mao Thana, border town *(author)*

LIST OF ILLUSTRATIONS

The *Pung cholom* (*author*)

Dancers of the Jawaharlal Nehru Manipur Dance Academy (*author*)

Memorial to the murdered British in the grounds of Raj Bhavan, the Governor's residence, Imphal (*By kind permission of Ayai Shimray*)

Maharajah Churachand's palace today (*By kind permission of William Clark*)

'The Civil Service in India seems to me a bad judge of a general policy. Their interests and prejudices are in favour of war and against the natives and to their own minds interest and prejudices seem to make up a principle. The difficulty is that they are the only people who know India, and one is led sometimes to think that there must be something in what they say. It would never do to let the government of India slip into the hands of natives (for none of them are really loyal to us. How can they be?) but many things will go smoother if worked by natives and the sense of injustice will be lessened...'

Letter from Benajamin Jowett, Master of Balliol College, Oxford, to Jessie Ilbert in India 9 September 1883.

From The Ilberts in India: An Imperial Miniature, by Mary Bennett, BACSA, London, 1995.)

Foreword

Ethel's portrait hangs in our house, and therefore I am reminded of her daily. My interest in her began with my search for the portrait, painted by my great-grandfather, the Victorian artist John Hanson Walker, who had exhibited it at the Royal Academy in 1892. The catalogue intriguingly described her as 'wearing the V.C.' It was not, I discovered, the Victoria Cross but the Royal Red Cross, personally given her by Queen Victoria at Windsor for her bravery in 'the Manipur disaster'. Ethel's own lively account of her time in India, *My Three Years in Manipur*, has been my inspiration for writing about her, although I realise that nothing can equal her own first-hand account of her ordeal. She was, like many Victorian women, physically tough, able to ride the extremely long distances and endure the discomforts involved in travelling in northeastern India at the time, and yet, in other respects, very reliant on her husband, who was several years her senior. Her infatuation with Tikendrajit, Prince of Manipur, whose overthrow of the Maharajah led to her husband's murder, is a fascinating aspect of the story, as is the passion with which the Queen threw herself into the whole affair.

It has been deeply interesting researching the background to Ethel's story, and a particular privilege to have been able to visit Manipur with the British Legion and see the cemeteries and battlefields of General Slim's 14th army—where action took place over the territory the Grimwoods had known so well. My thanks, too, to the Assam Rifles, who were generous hosts to us and guarded us on our way.

There is still a great deal I do not know about Manipur, and much that we missed, such as a chance to see one of their great festivals, like the shaman-led 'Lai Haroba', so I hope the reader will forgive me for any mistakes I may have made, and indeed will inform me of them. The spelling of Indian names and words varies a great deal in books and documents, so I have, in general, copied those used by Ethel herself or *The Times* newspaper.

One of the best things about writing books is the friends one makes in doing so, and this has been no exception. I was initially helped over Grimwood family history by Marcus Macaulay, a descendant, and am also grateful to David Spiller, who gave me extra information after Marcus's sad death. A special source of help was Edward Lowe, who filled in the story of Ethel's last years, and Colonel Promit Roy, who photocopied his extremely rare copy of Surendra Nath Mitra's *The Manipur War* for me while we were in Manipur.

Technology has sped ahead while I have been writing this book, and I am particularly grateful to those who have given me information by email, such as George Buermeyer, who knew that part of Oregon where Ethel settled, and sent me a lovely description of it. My thanks also to the many long-suffering librarians whom I asked for help, particularly those in the India Office of the British Library, who have been wonderful about supplying answers to my questions in record time. Websites, too, have proved invaluable, particularly Manipur's own excellent ones—a great help when letters take months to arrive, and often fail to do so at all!

As to the illustrations, I owe a great deal to Marcelle Adamson, librarian of the *Illustrated London News* Picture Library, for the use of the work of their brilliant band of artists who covered the disaster in 1891: I was amazed to find how accurate their drawings were. Also to Dr Stephanie Roy Bharath for her help in showing me the wonderful photographs in the Alkazi Collection. I am most grateful, too, to Dr Nimai Singh, Secretary to the Governor of Manipur, who gave me photographs and information on the memorial to the British in the garden of the Raj Bhavan. My thanks, too, to Ayai Shimray, our excellent guide while we were in Manipur, who very kindly also sent me photographs and

FOREWORD

information, and to William Clark, leader of our expedition. My especially warm thanks to Somi Roy, who not only has lent me his valuable family photographs, but has helped and encouraged me along the way while he himself has been busily engaged in film making and promoting Manipuri culture and projects for the good of his country.

I am particularly pleased to be being published once again by Book Guild Publishing, and greatly appreciate all the trouble they have taken over every aspect of the book.

Lastly, a very heartfelt thank you to my husband, without whose editing skills and interest I could never have completed this book.

Belinda Morse
27 March 2008

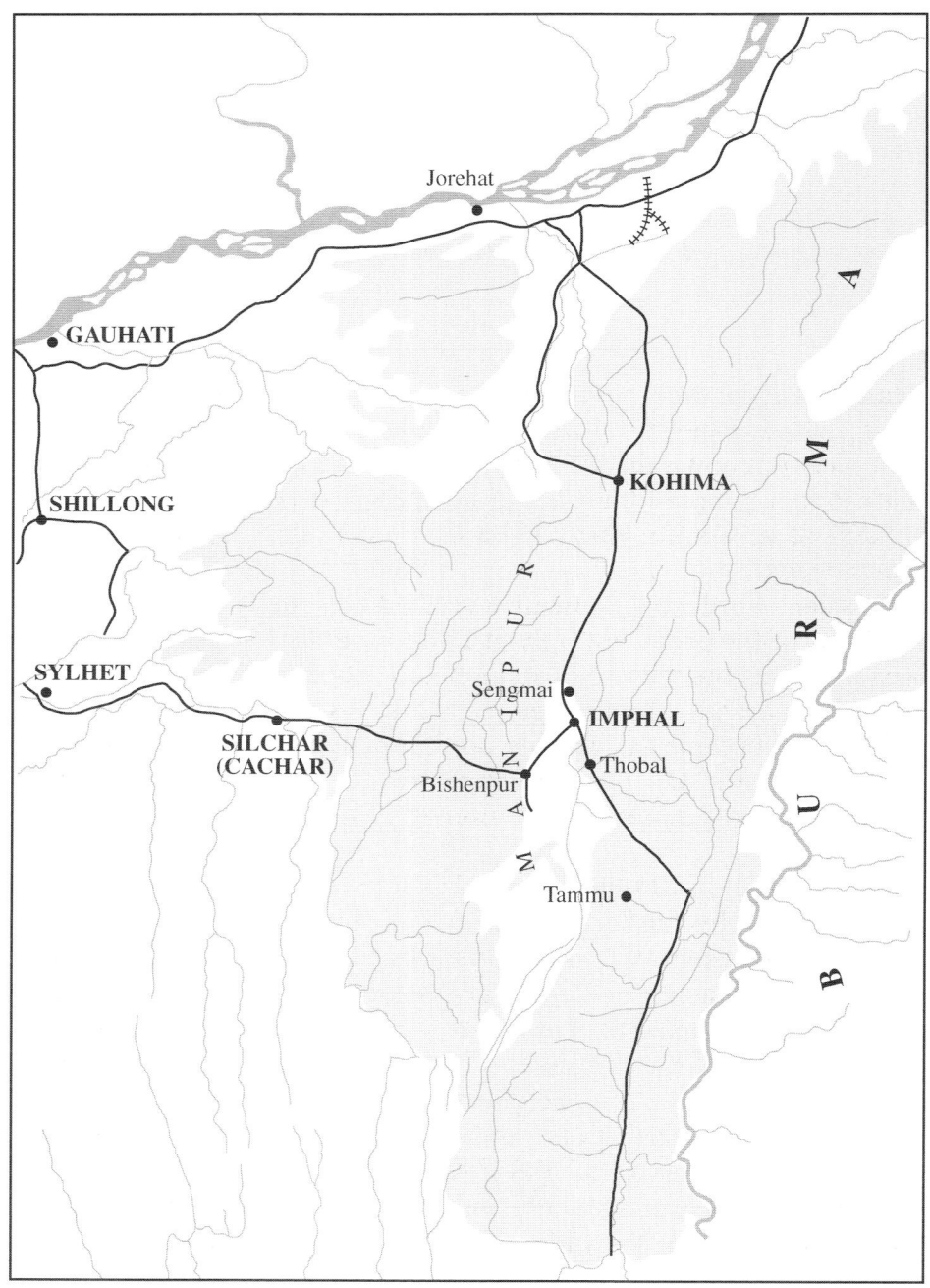

Note: Ethel referred to both the country and its capital Imphal as 'Manipur'.

1

A Posting to Manipur

'Manipur! How well I remember the first time I ever heard the name,' wrote Ethel Grimwood in 1891, 'a name that was comparatively unknown three short years ago, owing to the fact that it belongs to a remote little tract of country buried among hills and difficult of access, far away from civilised India, and out of the beaten track.'[1]

Between April and September 1891 Manipur dominated the headlines of the press, not only in London, but also in New York, because it was the scene of a sudden and tragic rising by members of the Maharajah's family against the British. It was a rising of which Ethel became the heroine, so that by the time she published her account of it *My Three Years in Manipur* the same year, hers was a household name, to be uttered with admiration but also pity.

Ethel arrived in Manipur in 1889 as a young 21-year-old newly married wife. Her husband, Frank, at 37, as so often in Victorian times was considerably older than her. After a conventional education at Winchester College and Merton, Oxford, to which he gained a Mathematical Postmastership, and where he rowed stroke for the college, Frank had been admitted to Lincoln's Inn as a barrister. By the time he married he had decided on a career change and had successfully taken the open examination to join the Indian Civil Service as a Political Agent.

Ethel's family were already deeply involved in India, either through the army or the Indian Civil Service, in which her father,

---

[1] *My Three Years in Manipur*, Ethel Grimwood, 1891.

Charles Moore, was a judge. She was his eldest daughter, and had been given the distinguished second name of Brabazon in recognition of the marriage of her great-grandfather John Moore to Barbara Brabazon, daughter of the Hon. William Brabazon, second son of the Earl of Meath.

Almost as soon as their fashionable wedding on 19 July 1887 at St Peter's, Cranley Gardens, Kensington was over, the Grimwoods had set off for India, where Frank had been appointed to a junior position in Sylhet, Western Assam. This proved a dull place for both of them, so that when after a few months he was offered the post of Political Agent in Manipur, a native state in the northeast often referred to as the 'jewel of India',[2] he jumped at the opportunity.

At that time only 60% of India was directly under the charge of the Viceroy or Governor-General. The rest of the country was made up of over 550 'native' or 'princely' states, each nominally under an Indian head of state or Maharajah, who recognised British sovereignty. Manipur was one of these, and had been associated with the British since 1823, when, following years of continual warring with Burma, a combined Manipuri/English force had successfully driven out Burmese invaders who had ousted the Maharajah and royal family. Following further land deals with the Manipuris in exchange for military help, the British had in 1835 installed a Political Agent in Manipur without, it seems, any formal treaty being made, but with the understanding that they would protect the ruler from foreign invasion. From then on the Maharajah governed with the advice of the Political Agent, who was appointed to his court by the Viceroy—in Frank Grimwood's day, Lord Lansdowne. Relations between the rulers of the native states and the British differed widely, some rulers remaining practically independent sovereigns, although all governed with the proviso they did not make war on other states or form alliances with foreign countries.

The Political Agent's role was diplomatic, and the job tended to be given to those who were well-mannered and able to keep a

---

[2] By tradition a magic jewel came into the possession of an early ruler.

good balance between their dealings with the government in Delhi and the ruling family of the state. Frank, the good-looking second son of a landed family of Essex and Wiltshire, seemed an ideal candidate for the job.

In going to Manipur, the Grimwoods were to find themselves in a far-flung state consisting of a fertile upland valley some thirty-six miles long by eighteen miles across, surrounded by hills, those in the north rising from five to six thousand feet towards the distant peaks of the Himalayas. The valley itself was one of a chain connecting Assam to Burma.

The *Assam District Gazetteer* of the time gives a vivid description of what it was like to arrive in the country:

> the traveller who enters Manipur by the Cachar road obtains a magnificent view of the valley from the summit of the Laimatol hill. For several days his path has lain across range after range of mountains, covered with forest so dense that he can seldom see more than a quarter of a mile ahead of him. Suddenly all is changed—the eastern face of the hill as it slopes before him to the valley is covered with short grass and rolling downs which take the place of the dense tropical forest. The valley lies before him like a map—at the north end some 20 miles away, are the dark green groves that conceal the town of Imphal. Elsewhere are level rice fields, and land covered with grass, about which are dotted the clumps of trees that mark the scattered villages. The Logtak lake sparkles in the sun and on every side the view is bounded by hills whose elevation is 2,600 ft.[3]

Imphal, Manipur's capital, was then no more than a collection of villages grouped together, with the Maharajah's fort and palace enclosure or 'pât' at its centre—its name being a corruption of 'Yumphal' or 'place of many dwellings'. As it was not a town in the European sense, Ethel always referred to it as 'Manipur' without making any distinction between town or state.

The Grimwoods were to learn that Manipur, strategically important to the British in guarding the security of the north-east frontier, had a distinctive life of its own, having existed as a kingdom from very early times. It had always been an unsettled

---

[3] *Assam District Gazetteer*, vol. IX, Baptist Mission Press, 1905.

2. 'A Naga house in Manipur': an illustration from one of the many weekly articles on the 'Manipur Disaster' which appeared in *The Illustrated London News* from April to September 1891. *(Illustrated London News Picture Library)*

country, not only because of its wars with Burma, but also because the area was very tribal, with as many as twenty-nine different tribes inhabiting it. To many of the British, Manipur's fame rested largely on its special breed of ponies, which in the past had made the formidable Manipuri cavalry feared throughout upper Burma, and which had led to the invention of the game of polo in the state. The thought of this thrilled Frank, who had paid a brief visit there once before, and had played a 'never-to-be-forgotten game of polo with three Royal princes on a ground worthy of Hurlingham'.[4]

In the Grimwoods' time the Manipuris, largely descended from Tibeto-Burman stock, had the reputation of being stalwart, industrious, energetic, and gifted with an aptitude for acquiring new arts. They were not naturally courageous, but capable of

---

[4] *My Three Years*, Grimwood.

fighting well, if well led. The women were particularly strong, and were cheerful, good-humoured, and famous for their weaving.

As the Grimwoods set off on their journey they may not have been aware that they could be heading into trouble, and that an Indian Secretary had once gone as far as exclaiming, 'Manipur is the Cinderella among political agencies—they'll never get a good man to take it.'[5] Earlier, in 1877, Captain Durand, the then Political Agent, had drawn a gloomy picture of the country, with misgovernment by the Maharajah, wretched conditions among the people, and the uncomfortable position of the Political Agent, whom he described as 'a British officer under Manipur surveillance ... surrounded by spies'.[6] This was because the Manipuris lived in fear of being annexed by the British, and therefore viewed the agent with deep suspicion.

Major General Sir James Johnstone, the very able and well-respected Political Agent who followed Durand, described the state's government as 'pure despotism tempered by assassination and revolution'. 'While he occupies the throne,' he wrote, 'the Rajah is perfectly absolute ... yet with all this power an obscure man may suddenly spring up, as if from the ground, to assert himself to be of the blood royal, and gathering a large party round him place himself on the throne. All this happened not infrequently in days gone by, when many were the rajahs murdered or deposed.'[7] Johnstone had personally found the Maharajah he served, Chandrakirti Singh, to be a loyal and helpful ally to the British Government.

In *My Three Years in Manipur*, Ethel describes the arduous sixteen-day journey she and Frank had to make in order for him to take up his appointment. They started from Sylhet in Assam, and rode eastwards on horseback, rising at 6 o'clock each morning to embark on fifteen miles of rough riding up and down what seemed endless ranges of steep hills through all weathers. Their nights were spent in leaky rest houses, where they would

---

[5] *My Experiences in Manipur and the Naga Hills*. Major General Sir James Johnstone, 1896.
[6] Ibid.
[7] Ibid.

often wait until the early hours of the morning for their luggage (which followed by elephant) to catch them up. Part of the journey was made along the Surma river in a small boat resembling a Noah's Ark, whose roof of coarsely woven bamboo matting was so low that they had to crawl under it to get into their sleeping bags, having awkwardly shuffled into their night clothes first.

The coolies the Grimwoods had hired to carry their baggage complained bitterly of the weight of their trunks, and finally ran away, so new porters had to be found. Having learned their lesson they took the precaution of keeping these in front of them, so as to avoid any further disappearances!

At last they reached Silchar, a small station twenty-four miles from the Manipur frontier, and about one hundred and thirty miles from Imphal. Here they broke their wearisome two weeks' travel. Silchar, in the neighbourhood of Cachar, was a centre for the tea-planting community, a small place which quartered a regiment. As was usual with the arrival of any newcomers in remote areas, the Grimwoods were welcomed warmly, and were able to lead a social life for three days before setting off again on the last eight-day stage of their journey. This involved crossing the Jhiri river, which formed the frontier between Manipur and British India. To Ethel, the most frightening part of their travels was having to cross rivers by means of bamboo suspension bridges. These were made of wire twisted into thick ropes stretched from trees on either side of the water, the railings being formed by bamboos fastened to the floor. These flimsy-looking bridges, though strong, hung perilously high over the water, and swung violently just as anyone reached the middle, so that it was difficult to keep a foothold.

Once they were in Manipur the road became potholed, and ran through dense forest jungle. It was April, and muggy, and they found themselves tormented by horseflies, gnats and heat. Their one relief was to be able to hand their baggage over to the local Nagas. Although they were fine-looking, Ethel found the appearance of these hillmen alarming. 'They wore very few clothes, and their necks were adorned with many necklaces made

3. An old suspension bridge in N.E. India of the kind that Ethel found very awkward to cross! *(The Alkazi Collection of Photography)*

of gaudily-coloured glass beads. Their ears were split to a hideous extent, and in the loops thus formed they stuffed all kinds of things—rolls of paper (of which they are particularly fond), and rings of bamboo, which stretched them out and made them look enormous.'[8]

They now had a guard of Manipuri sepoys[9] who marched ahead of them and helped to lead their horses through the deep mud which covered the road. At last they came to the final range of hills lying between them and Imphal. These hills rose to 6,000 feet in places, and the rough track over them was covered with bamboo jungle. Occasionally they passed a village, and every five miles or so a 'thana' or Manipuri look-out.

---

[8] *My Three Years*, Grimwood.
[9] Soldiers or policemen in India during British rule.

HEAD OF A NAGA CHIEF ON THE BORDER OF MANIPUR.

4. Head of a Naga chief from the borders of Manipur 1891. *(Illustrated London News Picture Library)*

The Grimwoods came to the final ridge at last, and saw the Manipur valley lying below them—a promised land looking calm and prosperous in the afternoon sun. Far away they could see the white walls of the Maharajah's palace, with its golden-roofed temple beside it, while villages surrounded by groves of bamboo and plantain trees dotted the plain, together with rice fields. Seventeen miles out of Imphal their party was met by the customary Manipuri guard of honour of fifty sepoys under their colonel, Samoo Singh, a high officer of state, who presented them with baskets of fowls and vegetables, and escorted them to the rest house. Suddenly they became conscious of their appearance, feeling they should appear smart for this last part of the journey,

5. A hillside village in N.E. India in the 1870s: typical of many villages still seen in Manipur today *(The Alkazi Collection of Photography)*

at the end of which they would meet the princes. Alas! Disaster struck when they realised that rats had eaten a large hole in Frank's hat and attacked Ethel's gloves! They were now ceremonially mounted on elephants decorated with bright red cloths for the last part of their journey. Seven miles out of Imphal they were met by four of the royal princes, and again taken to a reception area, where they were presented with even larger quantities of fowls, ducks and vegetables.

There were eight royal princes in Manipur, the former Maharajah having had six wives, all of whom had produced sons. Each prince held a special position in the court hierachy. Of the four who met them they took at once to Tikendrajit, the third son, who was the 'Senapati', or head of the armed forces. He was slim, with dark piercing eyes and a fair complexion. 'We liked what we saw of him on this occasion, and thought him very good-natured looking,' wrote Ethel.[10]

The Grimwoods rode with the princes into the town to a salute of twelve guns, then leaving them at the palace gate, turned towards the Residency, which had been built just outside the palace enclosure at the Maharajah's request, and was surrounded by a mud wall and ditch. It stood in spacious grounds, thanks to the former Political Agent Johnstone, who, when rebuilding it in 1880, had insisted that the site was entirely cleared of its poor surroundings.

The Residency was a large and pretty building with a thatched roof, constructed in the half-timbered style of an old English country house, though modified to suit the climate. It was built on one level over a substantial basement. This ensured that the rooms above were dry, and provided a guard room and storage space below. It had been made bullet-proof, which had at the time seemed to Johnstone unnecessary. 'Little did I dream that folly and incompetency would ever lead to our being attacked,' he wrote.[11]

Ethel's first impression as they approached the house was favourable. The drive was shaded by trees on either side, and beyond were stretches of grassland planted with deodars and flowering shrubs. The grounds included a tennis court, 'tanks'[12] and a lake with ducks. The Residency had a porch covered with a brilliant purple bougainvillea, and was surrounded by an English-style flower garden, divided off from the outer grounds by a hedge of blossoming cluster roses. The red-coated servants waiting at the door to greet them, together with two Gurkha orderlies, impressed Ethel, and made her think favourably about what their future lifestyle might be.

Shortly after their arrival a durbar, or meeting, was arranged at the Residency for their formal introduction to the Maharajah. For this the verandah and front steps were covered with red cloth,

---

[10] *My Three Years*, Grimwood.
[11] *My Experiences in Manipur*, Johnstone.
[12] These tanks were artificial freshwater ponds or reservoirs.

and their escort of sixty Gurkhas was drawn up on the lawn. The Maharajah, Surchandra, attended by his seven brothers, arrived with a large retinue of sepoys and ministers. Ethel described him as a 'short, fat, ugly little man with a face that looked a mixture of a Burmese and Chinese, much scarred by smallpox ... he was dressed entirely in white—a white coat with gold buttons and a fine white muslin Dhotee. He also wore a white turban, which was decorated with a spray of yellow orchids.'[13] The durbar ceremony only lasted ten minutes, and at the end the Maharajah requested to be introduced to Ethel, whom he obviously thought as odd a sight as she did him, for she found him staring at her as if she was some kind of strange animal.

Life at the Residency soon settled into a gentle routine, as the work of a Political Agent in a quiet place like Manipur was not too onerous. Among Frank's few responsibilities were trying disputes, checking revenue documents, sitting on district boards and committees, and generally keeping law and order among the tribesmen, whose raids and dacoities caused constant disruption.

The Grimwoods' day started with a ride each morning before breakfast, directly after which they would make a round of the stables and kitchen garden, feeding the little menagerie of animals that they had collected. For company they were dependent on the princes, whom they got to know well; Frank proved the perfect candidate for this ambassadorial part of the job, delighting in polo and all sports. He played polo frequently with the royal family, while Ethel rode with them. She was obviously very taken by Tikendrajit, the Senapati. She wrote:

> There was something about him that is not generally found in the character of a native. He was manly and generous to a fault, a good friend and a bitter enemy. We liked him because he was much more broad-minded than the rest. If he promised a thing, that thing would be done, and he would take the trouble to see himself that it was done, and not be content with simply giving the order. He was always doing little courteous acts to please us. I mentioned to him that I had been very much frightened by a lunatic in the bazaar ... I noticed after speaking to the

---

[13] *My Three Years*, Grimwood.

Senapati about him that he had not been at the bazaar for a long time, and afterwards I was told that the Prince had ordered him to be kept at home in the evenings, at the time we usually went out for a walk.[14]

Ethel mentions that the Senapati was not only a keen sportsman but also a brilliant shot. He particularly excelled at polo, which was played on the small shaggy local ponies, and Ethel was very impressed by his prowess, recording that he was a magnificent rider, who could send the ball skimming right across the ground with one hit. She also admired the picturesque clothes he wore when playing—a green velvet zouave jacket edged with gold buttons, a salmon pink silk dhotee, with white leather leggings, and a pink silk turban.

6. Manipuri polo players of 1891 seated on their small mountain ponies and wearing their special turbans or 'koiyets'. *(Illustrated London News Picture Library)*

---

[14] *My Three Years*, Grimwood.

In cold weather the Senapati would organise a week's deer-shooting for Frank in which Ethel would join, and for which they would ride on elephants. Very occasionally a tiger hunt was laid on, which was such a special event that the whole royal family would take part in it.

The royal princes, particularly the Senapati, would frequently visit the Residency informally, bringing with them a small following who would be left outside on the verandah while they went into the drawing room to look at Frank's photographs and inspect his guns, in which they took a keen interest. On other occasions the Senapati (who had several wives) would bring his young royal princesses with him, and they would run all over the house, examining everything, trying on Ethel's clothes and hats, and doing their hair with her brushes. They would then go into the garden to pick flowers, and Frank would photograph them. This photography was not to go unnoticed, and caused some suspicion.

On one occasion Ethel mentioned that she had never seen a shell fired, so the Senapati arranged a special field day, in which he brought out the army's two mountain guns, which he fired himself—every shot, she noticed, taking effect. These two 7-pounder guns, Enfield rifles and a quantity of ammunition had been given to the Rajah in celebration of the Queen's Golden Jubilee in 1887, and it would have been part of Frank's job to supervise and inspect the ammunition kept in the palace magazine, and check that it tallied with the books.

Another duty of the Political Agent was to learn the local language, so Ethel and Frank struggled, as she records, to learn Manipuri from the self-styled 'Burmese interpreter to the Political Agent'. Although schooled in England, Ethel spoke Hindustani, and proved an apt pupil. Her progress was such that their teacher showered her with compliments, which annoyed Frank and led to his somewhat humourless comment that they would take their lessons at different times in future.

After only ten months in the Residency, Frank was upset to learn that he was to be replaced by a more senior man, a Mr Heath, who was returning to India after being away on furlough.

It was a bitter moment for both Frank and Ethel. Whether there had been doubts about his ability at this stage is not revealed—his life so far had been easy and uneventful, and his limited experience of government not fully tested. With heavy hearts he and Ethel set off on the long journey to Jorehat, in the Assam valley, near the Brahmaputra, some two hundred miles from Manipur, which would take about three weeks to reach. They were accompanied out of the state by the eldest son of the Thangal General. The Thangal, who headed the armed forces, was one of the most powerful men in the country, despite being 85. Ethel described him as having deep-set glowing eyes and the expression of an eagle. He had been a clever engineer and bridge and road builder, and had worked closely with Johnstone, who admired him, but also credited him with having caused more bloodshed than any other man in the kingdom.

After a brief ten days in Jorehat the Grimwoods were posted on to Gauhati, arriving there in early April. Only a week later they heard that their successor, Mr Heath, was very ill with dysentery. Within days he was dead, and Frank was asked to return to Manipur.

2

A Palace Coup

Although she had been happy at Manipur, describing it as 'a pretty place, more beautiful than many of the showplaces of the world',[1] the prospect of their return there filled Ethel with dismay, particularly the thought of being back in the house where poor Heath had so recently died. Having to undertake the arduous journey again also daunted her. 'It was with a heavy heart that I superintended the arrangements ... an indefinable dread seemed to predominate over all I did,'[2] she afterwards wrote. To relieve some of the tension which may have arisen between them, and to cheer her up, Frank decided she should stay in Shillong for a few months. It was the headquarters of the British administration in Assam, and a delightful hill station situated among pine woods and waterfalls, with an ideal climate. Although she claims to have had a quiet time there, the naturally gregarious Ethel enjoyed it to the full, particularly because, it is said, she had the company there of her half-brother, Captain Alan Maxwell Boisragon. He was 30, in the Royal Irish Guards and a good athlete. He had recently returned to India after taking part in the Nile Expedition of 1884–85. Society in the hill stations was rife with gossip, and Ethel was later accused of having been too close to Alan, and too long away from the Residency.

Frank's love of photography also got him into trouble, leading to wild rumours about his conduct while Ethel was away. His enemies spread word that he kept a boat on the Residency tank in

---

[1] *My Three Years in Manipur*, Ethel Grimwood, 1891.
[2] *Ibid.*

which he played about with the local girls and took seductive photographs of them. He and a Lieutenant Simpson who was staying with him were also both accused of having had relations with the Thangal General's daughter.

Ethel had been away nine months when she returned to the Residency in November 1890. She felt unsettled, particularly by the sight of Heath's grave, which her bedroom window overlooked, and the fact that the officers and men of the nearby Langthabal fort had been moved away. She could not stop herself brooding on the remark she had overheard a friend make to her husband: 'What an unlucky place Manipur is! I have seen so many Political Agents go up there, and something always seems to happen to them.'[3] It was true that all three of Frank's immediate predecessors had met an untimely end. As a distraction, Ethel rode all over the country, getting to know the local geography well, which was to stand her in good stead later on. She feared nothing on these rides, but was not happy left alone at the Residency while Frank was away, feeling unsafe, despite being guarded by her old ayah, who slept on a mat outside her bedroom door.

Before Ethel's earlier departure from Manipur there had already been rumours of quarrels among the royal family—particularly between the Maharajah, his brothers and the Senapati. These were often petty, and sparked by small jealousies, such as who would win the favours of Maipakpi, a local teenage beauty, or even the Grimwoods themselves.

Although Surchandra, the Maharajah, seemed to be safely on the 'Gâdi', or throne, he was basically a weak man, unable to cope with the quarrels among his brothers. The worst of these were between his second brother, the Pucca Sena, and a younger one, Zillah Singh. Matters came to a head when the Pucca Sena managed to get the Maharajah to punish Zillah Singh by depriving him of his offices of state and place in the durbar. Zillah Singh took revenge by allying himself with the Senapati, Tikendrajit, to plot a coup.

---

[3] *My Three Years*, Grimwood.

A PALACE COUP

At 2 a.m. on the night of 20 September 1890, two months before Ethel's return, Frank was woken by the sound of gunfire. Two of the younger princes, with a handful of followers, apparently incited by the Senapati, had climbed into the Maharajah's apartments at the palace and fired shots through his window. He was not a courageous man, and fled immediately to the Residency in a state of panic, together with one of his full brothers. At dawn two more brothers and other officers, together with some 2,000 men, several of them armed, arrived to join the Maharajah, now under British protection. In a serious situation such as this Frank's duty was to decide whether extra troops should be called for. This put him in a very awkward position. If he immediately summoned up a military detachment to guard the Residency, the situation might get out of control. Instead, to the Maharajah's dismay, he ordered his officers' arms to be seized, saying they would only be returned when they dispersed. He then telegraphed the government for further advice. The instructions he received were to protect the Residency and to endeavour to mediate between the participants, it being stressed that anything he did must be purely defensive. Having taken these precautions, Frank tried to reason with the terrified Maharajah, urging him to make an effort to regain his throne, but nothing would persuade him to do so. Instead he became wary of Frank's intentions, and began to delude himself that he was conniving with the Senapati, the author of the coup, against him.

Failing to get the hoped-for support from the British, the Maharajah wrote to the Senapati formally abdicating in favour of his second brother, Kulachandra, the Jubraj; in doing so he declared that he was going on a pilgrimage to the holy city of Brindaban on the Ganges.

Frank telegraphed the government, informing them that he had guaranteed the ex-Maharajah's safety, but had warned him that once he had abdicated he could not return to Manipur. He did not, however, take the precaution of making him sign a formal letter or statement of abdication. He received instructions to recognise Kulachandra as Regent *pending sanction of the government of India*. This last clause was to be a source of trouble later. Although only recognised as Regent by the British,

Kulachandra was immediately accepted by the Manipuri people as their new King.

Kulachandra had cunningly absented himself from Manipur during the coup. However, once Surchandra had abdicated he returned to accept the throne, making the Senapati his Jubraj or second-in-command. He continued to be called the Senapati, although Angao Sena, his younger brother, became the official commander-in-chief of the army.

Once safely in exile, Surchandra made a complete volte-face: he denied he had abdicated, and accused Frank of disarming his troops without his consent, thus preventing him from making any attempt to regain the throne.

On her return to Manipur after the coup Ethel noticed many improvements. Roads had been repaired, bridges built, and the people seemed more contented. Frank, too, was finding it easier to work with the remaining four members of the royal family rather than with all former eight, and relations remained friendly. At Christmas he naïvely entertained them with a magic-lantern performance, showing slides he had made himself from his own photographs.

Early in the New Year of 1891, the Grimwoods went north to the military base at Kohima to meet the Chief Commissioner of Assam, James Quinton, spending four days in his company, Frank being his deputy. Ethel described what a treat it was to be there and to socialise with her fellow countrymen. She and Frank invited Quinton and his daughter to pay a return visit to Manipur, but he excused himself, saying his tour would not allow him time to come so far out of his way.

Later in the month the Grimwoods went to Tammu, Burma, enjoying their ride through cool teak forests, with the mountain ranges rising around them. Ethel delighted in the Burmese love of flowers, and the people's way of placing vases of them in front of their gods. She also enjoyed the vibrant colours of the women's clothes, the quaintly carved chessmen, and shopping for silk. The Grimwoods discovered that another Englishman, an army officer called Grant, was living in Tammu, quartered there with part of his regiment. They called on him and found him bright and

7 Maharajah Kulachandra, the last monarch from the Karta dynasty, who was deposed by the British in 1891. *(By kind permission of the Maharaj Kumari Binodini collection.)*

cheerful, despite the loneliness of his surroundings. Ethel became fond of his company, and persuaded him to help her make a cake. It ended up as a cinder, and earned sarcastic remarks from Frank.

On returning to Manipur, they were joined at the Residency by two visitors: a Mr Melville, the elderly superintendent of the telegraph department in Assam; and Lieutenant Walter Simpson, of the 43rd Gurkha Rifles, who had returned to inspect some military stores. Ethel knew Simpson well, for they had met in Shillong, and she particularly enjoyed his company, as he, like herself, was a musician, and liked nothing better than being left alone to play the piano for hours.

Simpson arrived on 21 February. On the same day Frank was electrified to receive a telegram from Quinton, the Chief Commissioner, saying, 'I propose to visit Manipur shortly. Have roads and rest-houses put in order. Further directions and dates follow.'[4]

It was suspected that this sudden visit was to do with the ex-Maharajah, who was in Calcutta, begging the government to reconsider his case and help him regain the throne, of which he claimed he had been unjustly deprived. Since his abdication the government of India had let matters rest, and had done nothing about formally recognising Kulachandra in his place, despite the fact that Quinton had decided that the ex-Maharajah was too weak to return. Frank, too, had probably remembered the passage in the *Manual of Instructions to Officers of the Political Department of the Government of India*: 'He [the Political Officer] should leave well alone; the best work of a political officer is very often what he has left undone.'[5]

Having procrastinated over the matter of Manipur, on 24 January 1891 the Government of India finally resolved that action must be taken, and an intervention made to make it clear to the state who were the masters. Differences between the brothers must be settled on principles of justice, and therefore it was decided that Quinton, as Chief Commissioner, should visit

---

[4] *My Three Years*, Grimwood.
[5] *Manual of Instructions to Officers of the Political Department of the Government of India*, 1924.

A PALACE COUP

Manipur personally, 'for the purpose of making, and if necessary enforcing, a decision upon the merits of the case'.[6]

Quinton left Calcutta on 21 February with orders to remove the Senapati (whom the government of India viewed as the instigator of all the trouble) from Manipur, and recognise the Regent as the official ruler. How he was to do it was left to him to decide. He was merely ordered to 'take a sufficient force, *even though opposition may not be expected*, (my italics) and report for the orders of the Government of India the conditions which you propose to attach to the recognition of the present Jubraj'.[7]

Quinton, a shaggy-looking man with heavy eyebrows, moustache and kindly face, had spent most of his long years in the Indian Civil Service in north-west India, and therefore did not fully understand Assam, to which he had been appointed only two years previously. He proposed taking a small escort of 100 police and 50 sepoys with him to Manipur, but was corrected by Brigadier General Collett, who told him to take 200 men, and an officer of at least the rank of colonel. This was again over-ruled by the Adjutant General, who ordered him to take 400 men armed with Snider rifles under the command of a Colonel Skene. Collett had originally estimated that each man should take 90 rounds of ammunition, but on hearing that there was plenty in the Residency already, reduced it to 40 rounds.

Ethel was corresponding at this time with a Lieutenant Williams of the 43rd Gurkha Rifles, and wrote from the Residency on 2 March:

> We are all in no end of excitement as yesterday the Chief Commissioner wired to say he is coming here also Col. Skene with 200 men of the 42nd, and though we are in the dark as to what is really going to happen we think that they are bringing the Maharajah back with them, and there will be some fun here. The present regal community seem determined to resist. The Chief and he will be here about the 23rd we think. They have kept it very quiet if the Rajah is coming back, and these people know

---

[6] N.Archives WO 106/145.
[7] *The Times*, May 26, 1891, p. 9. Viceroy's Official Report.

nothing at present; but the telegrams have been so curiously worded that we have put two and two together.[8]

She wrote to Williams again on 12 March:

Excitement is tremendous here. The Chief Commissioner is to arrive on the 22nd and Col. Skene, six officers and 450 of the 42nd with him. We have not been told what they are coming for, but of course can guess. The Manipuris are in no end of a funk; but they say they mean to resist sooner than let the Rajah return. Today we hear that one of the Princes with 1,000 men is going out to Sengmai on the way to Kohima to meet the Chief Commissioner and force. What this means we cannot tell; but it looks like resistance, and if so, there will be a small battle on the road. Also we have had a wire to say that Mr. Gurdon[9] from Golaghat is coming ahead of the Chief. He is travelling as fast as possible, and gets here on Sunday. What he is coming for we cannot imagine, unless it is to collect all the information he can and go back to meet the others, as the Chief Commissioner seems to think that letters or telegrams are unsafe.[10]

Many stories afterwards circulated about the 'curiously worded telegrams' Ethel refers to. According to some sources they were written in Italian, while others said they read that 'a big tiger would be caught shortly in Manipur'.[11]

As Ethel reports in her letter, the Indians were terrified that the British were plotting to reinstall Surchandra as Maharajah, and began storing arms. Frank seems to have taken no special steps to warn Quinton, being himself still in the dark, as his letter to a friend shows:

My wife leaves for England on April 9, and I hope to be home for September. I am expecting every day now the Viceroy's decision whether the Maharajah is to come back or not. His brothers, who turned him out, are rather uneasy as to what the result may be. If the Viceroy decides he is to return, there will be a small scrimmage. I hope he won't come back.

---

[8] N.Archives WO 32/8400.
[9] Lieutenant Gurdon was Quinton's aide-de-camp.
[10] N.Archives WO 32/8400.
[11] Compilation from the *Pioneer* newspaper, 1891, Allahabad, BL, V2876.

A PALACE COUP

Not that the present lot are much better; a native Administration is a dreadful thing to have to do with. It seems impossible to improve it.[12]

Frank was worried enough about the outcome of Quinton's visit that he tried to persuade Ethel to leave on an earlier boat. Her apparently sudden decision to go, however, appeared as a bad omen to the princes, and they all begged her to stay. In the end she stayed, as about ten days before Quinton was expected, the Grimwoods learned that it was *not* his intention to bring the Maharajah back.

Ethel's main preoccupation now became the task of feeding the large party on their way, as local meat was scarce, and they themselves lived on duck and other birds. At length, in the absence of anything else, she got hold of a goat, which was carefully fattened in the Residency kitchen garden, until it disastrously died the evening before the visitors' arrival!

Lieutenant Gurdon had been sent ahead of Quinton to make the arrangements for his visit, and it was from him, it seems, that Frank first learned that the Senapati was to be arrested and deported. On hearing this news, he warned Gurdon that Tikendrajit would resist to the uttermost, and would not allow himself to be taken alive. Gurdon then asked Frank whether he could bring pressure on Kulachandra the Regent to arrest him, but Frank knew this would not be feasible. The Senapati was famous throughout Manipur for his strength and courage, so much so that it was claimed that when only 16 he would unhesitatingly face large tigers with only a sword in hand. The killing of tigers had become such a hobby with him that his father had nicknamed him 'Koireng'—'tiger-hunter'. Along with this, he had a sudden and violent temper, which had led to his being banished in 1881 from Manipur for brutally ill-treating some villagers. Again in 1888 the government of India had advised the Maharajah to banish him for similar offences. Anyone trying to arrest him would be dealing with a desperate man.

When Frank rode out on Saturday, 22 March to Sengmai, the

---

[12] Published in *The Times*, 16 May 1891, p. 9 col.A.

last halting-stage on the road from Kohima to Imphal, to meet Quinton, he learned more of the scheme to arrest the Senapati at a durbar at the Residency. The plan, which he was sworn to keep secret, was without precedent, and dismayed him, particularly as he himself was to make the arrest. He felt deeply hurt that his opinion had not been sought, and that the government's solution had not been communicated to him before.

While Frank was with Quinton at Sengmai, Ethel and Lieutenant Simpson went out for an evening ride, and on returning home were surprised to see a huge number of Manipuri sepoys swarming along the road and into the fort.

Lieutenant Gurdon was later to say that, despite their fears as to his intentions on seeing the large numbers of his escort, the Chief Commissioner was treated with great civility and attention by the Manipuris, first being met by the Thangal General, one of the highest officers in the state, and then by the Senapati with a guard of honour.

It was early in the morning of 22 March when Quinton finally rode into Imphal, accompanied by 200 men of the 44th Gurkhas under Captain Boileau and Lieutenant Brackenbury, and another 200 men of the 42nd, commanded by Colonel Skene. Ethel recorded the feeling of anticipation:

> the morning ... broke clear and beautiful over the valley. The place had never looked more lovely. Clusters of yellow roses blossomed on the walls of the house, and the scent of heliotrope greeted me as I went into the veranda to watch my husband start to meet Mr. Quinton. There was a delightful sense of activity about the place, and one felt that something of more than ordinary importance was about to take place; white tents peeped out from amongst the trees surrounding the house, and the camp prepared for the Sepoys stretched along under our wall at the end of the lake ... chairs were placed near the principal palace gate, and a carpet, and a table with flowers on it; and there were a great many Manipuri Sepoys lining the road by which he was expected to arrive.[13]

---

[13] *My Three Years*, Grimwood.

Quinton met Kulachandra, the Regent, outside the gates of the fort, and after a little conversation announced that a durbar would be held at the Residency that day at 12 noon, and that he expected all the princes to attend. Kulachandra later asked for a postponement, because it was a religious 'fasting' day, but Grimwood replied that he could do nothing, as these were Quinton's orders. Quinton's party had gone on to breakfast with the Grimwoods. During the meal Ethel noticed how quiet her husband was, and found out that he had been ordered to arrest the Senapati personally at the end of the durbar, an act which he felt to be a bitter betrayal.

Preparations for the durbar were careful. All doors to the durbar room were locked except the one by which the princes would enter, and guards were stationed in the grounds. Two lines of sepoys were formed up on the steps leading to the Residency veranda, and more armed troops placed behind the building.

Fifteen minutes before the durbar was due to start there was a hitch, as the head clerk and Manipuri interpreter had not finished preparing a Manipuri translation of the Viceroy's orders. It was still unfinished when at noon the sound of a band playing and conch shells being blown warned them that Kulachandra was on his way. Grimwood told the interpreter to go and tell him to delay his arrival. He came back with Kulachandra's request that he bring three regiments with him as escort. Grimwood's reply was that one was enough.

Not until after 12.20 pm was the translation completed. Skene and the British officers then assembled at the foot of the Residency steps to receive the Regent and follow him up to the durbar room. He arrived alone, with a retinue of 100 men armed with rifles and shields. Frank Grimwood moved forward, saying, 'Rajah, you were asked to bring the Jubraj [Senapati]—why has he not come?'[14] The Regent replied that he was ill. (Manipuri oral tradition has it that *both* the Regent and the Senapati were waiting together outside the Residency gate, and that Ethel sent a servant with a bunch of flowers to the Senapati with a message

---

[14] *Documents on Anglo-Manipur War 1891*, N. Khelchandra Singh, 1984.

hidden in them warning him that he was in danger.) Frank said that the Senapati's absence must be reported to the Chief Commissioner, as the durbar could not proceed without him, and left the Regent standing in the sun for an uncomfortable ten minutes while he went to consult Quinton. He returned to say that the Chief Commissioner would not see him without the Senapati. Kulachandra made a show of sending to summon him, and, tired of being kept waiting, asked to sit in the durbar room. Frank accompanied him there, but being called for by Quinton, asked Captain Boileau to take his place. Boileau later recorded that while chatting with him some of his staff, looking out of the windows, saw the sepoys posted at the back, and reported it to Kulachandra, who stamped his heel on the floor in annoyance.

8 The British Residency at Manipur, defended by the Gurkhas on the fateful day of March 24, 1891 *(Illustrated London News Picture Library)*

A PALACE COUP

The Senapati now sent his reply that he was too ill to leave his house, and therefore hoped Quinton would excuse him from appearing. The durbar was therefore postponed until 8 the following morning, Monday 23 March, it being impressed on Kulachandra that his brother *must* attend. This left him in little doubt that he was in danger.

3

Under Fire

The durbar having been abandoned, the visiting party had time to amuse themselves, although Colonel Skene ordered his troops to keep together and not wander about, in order to be available if needed.

One of the sights of Manipur was the unique 'women's bazaar' which took place just outside the west gate of the palace enclosure. The women of Manipur were famous for being hard-working and good at weaving. Besides labouring in the fields they ran the bazaar entirely on their own, allowing no man to sell there. The sight of hundreds of women sitting in long rows behind their vegetables, fish, foodstuffs, cloth and jewellery was popular with visitors, who would have also been interested in their dress—a long striped cloth with a border called a 'phanek', which was wound round their body from their bosom to their heels.

Quinton visited the bazaar in the afternoon with Ethel. Captain Boileau also went, and was struck by the unusually tense atmosphere—everyone appeared nervous. He wrote:

> While I was looking at it a procession came out of the west gate of the palace enclosure with banners and conch shells. Some women called out 'the Jubraj is coming'. Just then a bugle sounded in our lines—an ordinary bugle call. I think it was the guard bugle, and some of the sepoys who were in the bazaar at once ran towards the lines, on seeing which, a sort of panic ensued among the women, most of whom rose up and began

to run away. But a Manipuri who was with me shouted out 'It is nothing, only the Holi procession' ... on which they all quieted down again.[1]

That evening the officers dined in the Residency, and were entertained, as had been previously arranged, by the Regent's band. There were fifteen officers in all, making Ethel feel somewhat out of it as the only woman. The thought that Percy Melville, superintendent of the telegraph office at Kohima, was to leave the next day also saddened her, so she made him promise to delay his departure until the afternoon. In all other respects the evening passed off cheerfully enough, and at 11 p.m. the party broke up, and everyone went to bed.

The following morning they were up early in preparation for the durbar. At 8 o'clock, however, a message arrived from the Senapati saying he was too ill to leave his palace, and therefore Kulachandra, the Regent, would not come either. After a serious discussion it was decided to make a last attempt to persuade the princes to attend, and the durbar was postponed until 1 p.m.—but again no princes appeared.

In the early afternoon Frank and Ethel stood on the Residency steps to see Melville off to Kohima. Watching the coolies loading his luggage, they felt a sudden fear for him, not liking the present feeling of uncertainty. He was slightly crippled, and the thought that he was leaving without any escort to protect him bothered them, although he couldn't be persuaded to stay on.

Shortly after this, Frank, accompanied by Simpson, set off for the palace carrying a letter from Quinton ordering the Regent to give up the Senapati with the ultimatum that if he failed to do so the Chief Commissioner would be compelled to have him arrested. They found Kulachandra in a very nervous state, and in obvious fear of the Senapati. He begged for time, saying that he would consult his council for their advice and give his answer the next day. Frank refused to allow this, giving him just half an hour to reply. When the reply came it was to say that the council

---

[1] N/A WO 32/8400: *Proceedings of Court of Enquiry into Events of March 1891.* Holi: the Hindu spring festival.

considered the Senapati an innocent man, and would not therefore surrender him.

Negotiations in the palace had taken nearly three hours, and as Grimwood and Simpson left they were amazed to find it was now crowded with so many sepoys that it resembled a hornets' nest. The Regent explained this away by saying that they were gathering for a review planned as part of the welcome intended for Quinton and the other visitors.

On their way back to the Residency, Grimwood and Simpson came face to face with the Senapati, who, on orders from the Regent, had been carried down in a litter, having been assured that they had come alone. He seemed genuinely unwell, with a high fever. As he was known to suffer from gallstones, he may well have been suffering an attack at that moment. Despite this, Frank felt compelled to tell him of his proposed arrest and banishment, pointing out that it need not be permanent, but would depend on his good conduct.

Unusually, no bazaar was held that afternoon. At about 5 p.m. Captain Boileau was approached by two men who warned him that the Regent had collected a very large number of soldiers in the palace and meant to attack. They would be 'rushed' that night by Kukis and Nagas. This Boileau reported to Colonel Skene, who sent one of the men to Grimwood. Perhaps due to the tension caused by his failure to arrest the Senapati, the latter treated him roughly, calling him a 'badmash' (rascal), and had him locked in the guardroom.

It was decided that the only possible solution to the situation was to use force. At this, Ethel felt a wave of excitement sweep through the men, an emotion that chilled her. Already, she noticed, the town looked empty, and the main road, usually crowded with people, was deserted. At about 7 o'clock the skies darkened and a heavy thunderstorm broke. In order to try and combat her feelings of worry and confusion, Ethel decided to walk round the Residency and tidy the rooms. In doing so she found that many of their servants had fled, among them, to her dismay, her old ayah. This hurt her greatly, for she had at least, in this male-dominated place, been a fellow woman. When she returned, Ethel found Quinton and two of the other officers whiling away their time before dinner by playing whist. She then went into the kitchen, wisely taking the precaution of getting those that remained of her staff to prepare a large quantity of soup and cooked fowls, fearing that if there was action the next day the rest would flee.

Afterwards Ethel was to remember that dinner had been a quiet meal:

> I felt nervous and low-spirited, and very lonely, quite out of place amongst those men whose profession it was to fight: ... thoughts of England and of all whom I loved there, flocked through my mind, and I wondered what they would say if they could see us then, and know the possible danger that threatened us and our home. My husband was troubled at the thought of my being in the place at such a time, and he blamed himself for having agreed to my staying, though I had done so of my own free will.[2]

A Manipuri 'nautch', or dancing show, had been arranged to entertain the visitors after dinner. These traditional and graceful dances were an integral part of Manipuri social life. No dancers appeared, however, so Lieutenant Brackenbury did his best to enliven the atmosphere in their absence by playing his banjo and singing comic songs.

Colonel Skene had ordered all the British officers to the Residency after dinner to be briefed on the plan of action which he had drawn up, which was to surprise and seize the Senapati in his own palace in the early hours of the morning. A main party of 70 men under Captain Butcher was to 'rush' the Senapati's house, supported by Lieutenant Lugard and his troops, while Lieutenant Brackenbury was to guard the entrance to the palace should he try to escape. Lieutenant Chatterton was to capture and hold the west gate of the outer enclosure facing the Cachar road, thus guarding the camping ground of the visiting troops. Colonel Skene would wait at the camp with reinforcements.

---

[2] *My Three Years in Manipur*, Ethel Grimwood, 1891.

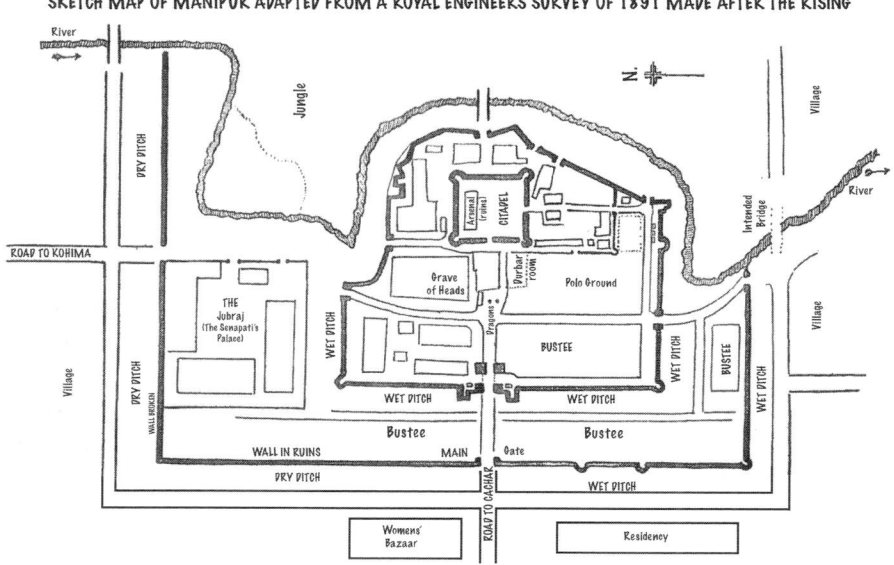

9 Plan of the Fort, Royal Palace and surroundings, 1891 adapted from R.E. Survey of 1891

After their visitors had retired, the Grimwoods went out into the garden. As they walked up and down in the moonlight, Frank tried to reassure Ethel, who felt restless and unhappy, that all would be well. They were just preparing to go in when they heard the sentry challenge someone at the gate. It was a Manipuri saying he had been sent from the palace to enquire whether they wished to have the nautch or not, as the dancers were waiting outside in the road. He was told that it was much too late, and was sent off. Afterwards they wondered if he was a spy. If so, he would not have gained much information, as all they had done at the Residency was to put on one or two extra sentries because of the Chief Commissioner's presence.

That night Ethel spent a sleepless few hours until finally, at 3 a.m., she woke Frank to give him a quick breakfast, before he joined Colonel Skene and the other officers. To her dismay he had decided to take part in the action; she had hoped that, being a civilian, he might remain out of it.

It was a bitterly cold night, and after Frank had left and while it was still dark Ethel accompanied Quinton and Cossins, his secretary, down to the telegraph office. This was at the end of the drive, about three hundreds yards from the Residency, and was in one of a pair of strongly built buildings which stood opposite each other. The second of these served as Frank's office and treasury.

Once in the telegraph office they wrote a message to the government of India giving details of the current situation, and were just handing it to the native clerk to send when they heard gunshots being fired at the Senapati's house, followed at once by others. The telegram remained half sent as a bullet hit the office window beside them, shattering the glass. Unnerved, Ethel took refuge in the stone basement of the building.

The British troops' orders were not to fire until fired upon, and to bring the Senapati, once captured, to the Residency. As planned, Lieutenant Brackenbury had moved off first, followed by Butcher. As Butcher's troops approached the Senapati's compound they were fired on. Although Butcher himself escaped, seven of his soldiers were wounded, and had to be carried to the upper storey of the nearby temple. Here 7-pounder guns were brought into action against them, about which they could do little, as the density of the surrounding buildings made it impossible to see from where they were being fired. This meant the temple had to become a medical post. News then reached them that Brackenbury, who had been guarding the entrance to the palace, had been badly wounded. Later it was said by the Manipuris that the British in their turn had killed some women and children, relatives of the royal family, in their attack on the palace. At about 9 a.m., Lieutenants Lugard and Woods returned to Skene to report on the action, whereupon Skene set off with a scaling ladder and some 50 men to try and rescue the wounded from the temple.

At 10.30 a.m. Frank called at the drive office to get some more ammunition, telling Ethel, who was still there, that he was afraid they would run short if they went on much longer. The problem was that his guard was armed with Martini-Henry rifles, whilst Quinton's men were equipped with Sniders, and the ammunition was not compatible. He explained that the Senapati's house had been captured, although only after a fight, but that the Senapati had not been found there. The main gateway was in their possession, but Lieutenant Brackenbury could not be found, and they did not know whether he was wounded or dead.

At about midday Ethel and Quinton managed to get back to the Residency. They had made further attempts to telegraph the government of India, but found that all the wires had been cut. Ethel organised tea and sandwiches, although it was difficult as those servants who remained were very frightened and demoralised. Afterwards she made a quick reconnoitre of the house, and was relieved to find that although a bullet or two had hit the walls, the building itself was not much damaged.

About an hour later Frank returned with Colonel Skene and some other officers. They were obviously worried about the situation, and particularly about the fate of Lieutenant Brackenbury. While they were lunching Frank asked Ethel to organise some food for the men who were still at their posts. Finding her remaining servants had fled, she went into a little room next to the dining room to cut sandwiches herself. Just as she was doing so a bullet cracked through the window above her head. Dropping the knife in terror, she rushed back into the dining room—only to find it empty. The officers had all gone, because it had been discovered that the Manipuris were attacking the Residency from the back. It took time to drive them off, as most of the troops were engaged in the palace area, and in the end they had to resort to setting fire to the nearby Naga village, which the Manipuris were using as cover.

By now the Residency was under fire from the front as well as the back. Ethel (who had refused to take to the cellar as her husband had suggested) wrote:

> It was heart-rending to see the work of destruction which was proceeding in the different rooms ... the windows were broken, and every now and then bullets crashed into the rooms, smashing different things—first a

picture, then a photograph. All my beloved household goods seemed coming to grief under my very eyes, and I was powerless to save them. We did try to collect some of the most valuable of our belongings together and put them away in a heap in the durbar room, which at that time had escaped with only one broken pane; but it was dangerous work going into the front rooms to remove them, for as the afternoon went on the firing became hotter, and bullets rained into the house at every second.[3]

As the afternoon progressed the situation became so bad that the decision was taken to withdraw. Captain Butcher was charged with posting all the outside troops into the Residency compound, a job which took a long time, and which allowed the Manipuris to shell the Residency to great effect from loopholes in the outer wall of the palace.

News came that Lieutenant Brackenbury had been discovered lying on the bank of the river north of the palace. He was badly wounded, having mistaken his direction and come under heavy fire, but by some miracle was still alive. The wounded had been collected and taken to the hospital, which was in the Residency grounds but a little way from the house. However, it was not bullet-proof, so Frank and Ethel set to work to bring blankets and sheets down to the Residency cellar so that they could be brought to its greater safety. As they did so shells were bursting overhead, making them fear that the thatch of the roof would soon be set alight.

Ethel wrote:

There were a good many of us in the cellar by this time—Mr. Quinton, Colonel Skene, my husband and myself, Mr. Cossins and Mr. Gurdon. It was about seven o'clock, and a lovely evening. The sun was just setting, and the red glow of the sky seemed to illuminate the landscape around and the faces of the colonel and my husband as they stood in the doorway talking together in low tones.[4]

The grim reality faced them that with only a few rounds of ammunition left, the Residency was untenable. What action

---

[3] *My Three Years*, Grimwood.
[4] *Ibid.*

should they take? Grimwood advised evacuating the building and falling back on the heights about one and a half miles distant from it, where they might be able to hold out until relieved. Skene, to Ethel's horror, agreed. Quinton, however, overruled them, deciding to first try and negotiate a truce. The bugles were sounded for a ceasefire, and were answered by a loud gong from the palace. The enemy's guns stopped, and as night fell, all was quiet.

Quinton now dictated a letter asking under what conditions the Manipuris would agree to end the hostilities. The answer, written in Bengali, came back at 9 p.m. It reminded them of the services rendered to the British by Manipur, then stated: 'If the British would lay down their arms then the Manipuris would not re-open hostilities.'[5] They found the exact meaning of the Bengali phrase unclear. Did it mean 'Surrender arms' or 'Cease fire'? Skene told Quinton that in no circumstances would he lay down arms, whereupon Quinton suggested they go and ask the Senapati in person to clarify his meaning. Lieutenant Chatterton afterwards recalled hearing Grimwood ask the messenger for a promise of safe conduct if Quinton went. The reply was, 'Yes, why should we harm you? Are you not our God?'[6] Grimwood and Simpson then went to the west gate and returned with the news that the Senapati would meet them there. Simpson turned to Quinton and said, 'Will you come out, sir—we think that terms can be made as the Jubraj [Senapati] has said he has had enough of it, and that he will meet you on the road.'[7] At this, Quinton at once prepared to go, calling to Cossins to accompany him. Skene and Grimwood, who asked Simpson to join him, followed. They went naïvely and trustingly without escort, even divesting themselves of their swords and revolvers before they left. They walked to the west gate, and talked for some time outside it with palace officials. Chatterton, who was watching, ordered some chairs to be taken

---

[5] *Queen Empress vs Tikendrajit*, John Parratt, 1992.
[6] *The Times*, June 4, 1891, p. 5, col. A.
[7] *Ibid.*

10 The Palace gates through which Commissioner Quinton and his party entered unarmed and vanished before their murder. *(Illustrated London News Picture Library)*

out to them before they disappeared into the palace through the main gate. Lieutenant Gurdon recalled:

> Time went on and we began to feel anxious as we watched the fort gate for any sign of our party returning. Still all remained quiet, and we could not tell what was going on. Our position was a difficult one. If we went to the gate to see why the Chief Commissioner did not return our conduct might be liable to misconstruction by the Manipuris. At last about midnight someone shouted out from the outer wall of the palace in Manipuri something like 'the Chief Commissioner will not return'.[8]

Almost immediately the firing recommenced. One gun was placed in an embrasure in the palace walls opposite the Residency and only 200 yards from it and the Manipuris had taken advantage of the ceasefire to infiltrate the Residency grounds.

---

[8] Viceroy's official report, *The Times*, May 16, 1891, p. 9, col. A.

Ethel had begged to be allowed to accompany Frank to the palace, but he had refused, telling her to stay with the others and keep a brave heart. She wrote:

> I remained where he had left me, alone for some minutes, though some of the officers were standing just outside the door of the cellar where I was sitting. It seemed so hard that I could not go with my husband. I feared being left alone without him, and felt very lonely and broken-hearted among so many men, mostly strangers to me.[9]

During the evening Calvert, the surgeon, helped by Lieutenant Lugard, who was shot in the leg doing so, brought the wounded into the Residency cellar from the hospital, which had become untenable. The surgeon afterwards wrote:

> the medical officer would like to call attention to the conduct of Mrs. Grimwood, the wife of the Resident. This brave woman had been under fire all day, her own room had been wrecked by shellfire, her husband had gone with the Chief Commissioner on a dangerous mission, and yet with a difficult withdrawal, or a still more hopeless prospect of attempting to hold out before her, she came down among the wounded after herself preparing soup, beef-tea, etc. and administered it to them, they having been without food all day. This enabled the medical officer and the hospital assistants to dress the wounded and begin operating.[10]

Ethel wrote her own account as part of a long letter to her sister-in-law, Mabel:

> I pray that I may never see such sights again. There were crowds of them, some dying. Poor Mr. Brackenbury was the first, shot all over, both legs broken, both arms, bullets in him all over the place, and yet, poor lad, he was alive and perfectly conscious the whole time, and in awful agony. I did what I could to help, but it seemed almost impossible to do anything. In one corner was a poor fellow with his brain shot out on the top of his head, and yet alive; another with his forehead gone, and many others

---

[9] *My Three Years*, Grimwood.
[10] British Library, India Office Records L/Mil7/15110, *Operations in Manipur 1891*.

worse. Luckily I am rather strong-minded, and so I was able to help in bathing some of the wounds and bandaging them up.[11]

Later Ethel scratched together some food for them all.

> Perhaps had we known that it was our last meal for nearly forty-eight hours, we should have taken care to make the most of it; but no thought of what was coming entered our minds, and long before the melancholy meal was ended most of the officers were dozing, and I felt as though I could sleep for a week without waking.[12]

She went again to the cellar, and found that Calvert needed milk, so returned to the dining room. Here, helped by Captain Boileau, she mixed condensed milk with water, and carried the jugs back to the cellar. Finding that the wounded had now grown quieter, she returned upstairs, intending to go to her room for some sleep. She walked, as she recalled, through the house as in a dream. When she reached the door of her room it would not open, for part of the roof had fallen in. Instead she retired to the verandah, where Captain Butcher was already dozing:

> I went down the steps and stood outside in the moonlight for a few minutes. It was a lovely night, clear and bright as day! One could scarcely imagine a more peaceful scene. The house had been greatly damaged, but that was not apparent in the moonlight, and the front had escaped the shells which had gone through the roof and burst all round the back. The roses and heliotrope smelt heavy in the night air, and a cricket or two chirped merrily as usual in the creepers on the walls.[13]

By now she was getting increasingly anxious about Frank, and was thinking of going to the gate to look for him when she came across Captain Boileau. Ethel later wrote, 'You will remember my asking you if you would mind going to look for him, and you went away at once to do so. You had not been gone many minutes

---
[11] Letter written from Lahkipur, Cachar April 2, 1891, RA VIC/N/47/175. By permission of Queen Elizabeth II.
[12] *My Three Years*, Grimwood.
[13] *Ibid.*

when I woke up from a doze on the front verandah to hear those terrible guns starting again.'[14] For a few minutes she could not stir. Terror had frozen her. She then rushed through the house down to the cellar and heard they had taken her husband, the Chief Commissioner and their whole party prisoners.

What happened next will never be clear. It was obvious to all that they did not stand a chance if they remained in the Residency. Boileau, the senior officer among them, appeared indecisive, but later claimed that several people, Ethel among them, had brought pressure on him to abandon the Residency. He took a vote, and it was decided unanimously that they should leave. Dr Calvert asked, 'Is it your order to go?' to be told, 'I have given no order.'[15] At that moment a volley of shots rang out from the stables, and a shell ripped through the house, leaving them no option but to quit.

To Ethel, their departure seemed to take an age, as all the wounded had to be carried out on to the grass outside. Brackenbury was brought out first, despite begging to be left in peace behind, but the move killed him, and he was taken back. Ethel covered him with a sheet before leaving. She almost envied him as he lay wrapped in the slumber of death which had taken his pain and suffering away.

---

[14] N/A WO 32/8400, Proceedings of Court of Enquiry, Manipur, 1891.
[15] *Ibid.*

4

A Torturous Escape

Outside the cellar all was confusion, and the noise deafening, shells bursting everywhere. About one hundred and sixty soldiers were gathered on the grass, together with large numbers of servants and followers. Boileau and Butcher were too distracted to make any serious attempt to muster their men, a sepoy later reporting that Boileau had come to them and said, 'Try to save your lives—how much ammunition have you got?'[1] They had none, having been 450 against a force of thousands.

Ethel recollected that she stood for some time watching people escape before the sudden fear took hold of her that she had been forgotten and left behind. She thought of going on, but remembered the officers had made her promise to stay where she was until fetched. She eventually left with Lieutenant Gurdon, just behind the front line. They were followed by the sepoys, who carried the wounded on their backs, whilst Captains Butcher and Boileau brought up the rear. Ethel was soon caught up in the mêlée of people rushing about and knocking each other over in their desire to escape. She wrote:

> Out in the open, away from the shelter of the house, with one's life in one's hands, as it were, my senses nearly left me. The noise was awful, for besides the bursting of the shells, the firing was heavier than it had been before. I had not gone six yards from the house when a shell exploded almost at my feet, knocking off some branches of a big tree close by, and wounding me very slightly in the arm. I jumped behind the tree, in the vain hope that its broad trunk might save me from further injury, and

---

[1] B/L, India Office Records L/Mil/7/15110: *Operations in Manipur, 1891*.

there I remained for some seconds. The scurrying of those going towards the river awoke me to my senses again, and off I went too, forgetting to look for my companion, from whom I had managed to get separated.[2]

She now had to scramble through a tall thorn hedge, which she herself had had planted in order to keep cows from getting into the flower garden, and which Frank had jokingly said would keep out an army. Fortunately part of it had already been broken down by those scrambling through before her. The next hazard was a low mud wall with a six-foot drop on the other side. A hand pushed her off from behind, and a friendly Indian helped her slither down to the muddy river bank below. The water was icy cold, but fortunately the stream was low enough to wade through. She had reached the middle and was standing there up to her shoulders when the surgeon, Calvert, caught up with her, and carried her to the far edge. Just as he reached the bank his foot slipped in the mud, and they both fell, causing Ethel to lose one of the heels of the flimsy house shoes she was wearing. She had had no time to collect any warm clothes before leaving, so was wearing only what she had had on during the day. Her serge skirt was now so sodden it dripped with water, and so heavy that some of its fastenings broke.

Scrambling up the opposite bank of the river, the party crossed a road. Once safely over, the order came to lie down in the deep ditch beyond to wait while the wounded were brought over. Ethel lay listening to the sound of firing, not being able to tell from whose side it came. She was to hide in several more ditches that night.

It was decided to make for the Cachar road, in the hope that they would intercept a party of the 43rd Gurkha Rifles, under the command of Captain Cowley, who were known to have begun a march to Imphal from there before the rebellion began, and were due to reach Leimatak, some thirty miles from the capital, that day.

Ethel recalled that the moonlight was still very bright:

---

[2] *My Three Years in Manipur*, Ethel Grimwood, 1891.

A TORTUROUS ESCAPE

> It was about two in the morning that we left the Residency, and we marched steadily on until daybreak. We had not gone four miles away from the station, when I turned to look back, and found the whole sky for miles round lit with a red glow, whilst from the trees surrounding our house flames were leaping up. Those only who have feelings of affection for the places where they live, and which they call home, can picture what that burning house meant to me. All we possessed was there—all our wedding presents, and everything that goes towards making a place homelike and comfortable.[3]

Ethel thought of her husband, whom she believed to be a prisoner in the palace, feeling that for the moment he was better off than they were. She believed that the Senapati would not only remember their friendship, but be clever enough to see the advantage of keeping the English as hostages.

The red glow of the flames lasted until they were swallowed up in the light of dawn. By this time the escaping party were on the Cachar road, and several miles from Imphal. They now made a halt to decide on the safest route to follow. Having been shot at at intervals along the way, they felt it would be safer to cut across to the hills and avoid Bishenpur, which was fortified. If all went well they would then strike the Cachar road at a higher point. Just as they were starting to move off a messenger caught them up and informed Boileau and Butcher that a large number of their men had been left behind in the Residency compound. It later transpired that nearly two-thirds of their troops had been left to their fate, without being given any orders. The officers turned a deaf ear, however, and marched on.

Ethel was exhausted, her arm bleeding, and her feet badly cut from the rough walking. As they marched, the sun beat relentlessly down on them, parching their mouths, but they could find no water that was drinkable. One of the officers lent Ethel his helmet to protect her from sunstroke, but all the time she thought she heard the sound of gunfire in her ears.

At last they reached the hills. Their first climb was very steep, up a bare slope covered with the rough stubble of the previous

---

[3] *My Three Years*, Grimwood.

year, which, as was the custom, had been burnt. The longer tufts hit them in the face, so that they got covered with soot.

By mid-afternoon they had reached a plateau about halfway up. From here they had a wide view of the plain, and were able to find shade and some fresh water. They slept for a while, but on starting again found they had a crowd of natives on their tail, waving their dhaôs (sharp, broad-bladed knives) and spears. Fortunately they kept a certain length behind, apparently fearful of being shot.

The party were now at about 2,600 feet, and aiming to reach a ridge some 2,000 feet higher. Ethel remembered that the Cachar road passed over the top of Leimatak hill, which, at 6,700 feet, was the highest peak of the first range lying between Imphal and Cachar. There was no path, and their ascent became so steep that they were reduced to crawling up on their hands and knees. Eventually they halted, having spotted a Naga village about 1,500 feet further above them. Leaving Ethel and the wounded at the foot of the ascent, a party made for the village and, finding it deserted, sent for the others to come up. There they halted for a while, and Ethel recalled that while they were resting a young Naga, who had been in their service as a 'sais' or groom, found them. He had risked being discovered by the enemy to present her with three eggs. She was greatly touched, but none of them could stomach the eggs, despite the fact that they had not eaten for twenty-four hours.

One of the officers had made a reconnoitre during their halt, and had come across a Manipuri thana. The guard had called out that he had orders to pass the Memsahib and sepoys, but that all the officers must turn back. As soon as he learned that he was not going to be obeyed, he set his men to fire on them. Lieutenant Lugard of the 42nd Gurkha Rifles takes up the story at this point:

> Parties (had) got separated, and by this time we were reduced considerably in strength, heavily impeded by the wounded whose sufferings must have been terrible, carried in blankets or on the backs of exhausted Kahars and Sepoys. Mrs. Grimwood must have suffered terribly—notwithstanding her terrible experience on the 24th the brave woman

11 Fugitives from the Manipur Residency fighting on the road during their retreat, as depicted by Richard Caton Woodville, one of the *Illustrated London News'* regular artists. *(Illustrated London News Picture Library)*

bore up throughout the desperately trying march, marching almost barefooted (as she only wore thin house slippers with fancy netted stockings which were soon torn to shreds), setting us all a good example.[4]

Lugard explains that finally, utterly exhausted, and without food or shelter, they halted under cover of some jungle, and got a few hours of broken sleep. According to Ethel, it was now about 1 a.m. The night was bitterly cold, so the officers lent her their greatcoats to sleep under, bearing the cold themselves. Thanks to them she slept soundly until they woke her at 3.30 a.m.

Lieutenant Lugard continues:

> We started again at daylight—the night having passed peacefully, though we heard the firing at some distance of one of our parties that had got separated. We struggled for a mile or so along a Naga path in search of the Cachar road. Having no food we began a diet of leaves, for we were not very hopeful of falling in with Captain Cowley's party ... [as] owing to the difficulty of carrying the wounded we only made about a mile an hour. We struck the main road after some two miles and finding no trace of elephants [Captain Cowley's transport] ... presumed he was still before us. We pushed on some distance with great difficulty, until we found it simply impossible to get the worst of the wounded forward. Our party was now too small to admit of splitting it up. It was decided that the best thing for all was to conceal in the jungle the three worst wounded and push on as rapidly as possible to join Captain Cowley, get help from him, and return for the wounded.[5]

After some distance they surprised a Manipuri piquet on the road: they were cooking, and fled. The half-cooked rice on the camp fire was greedily seized by them all. They took one of the Manipuris captive, and learned from him that Captain Cowley had not yet passed along the road, so that with luck they might still come across him. Their prisoner informed them that a large number of the enemy lay ahead, and advised them to take to the jungle again, offering to show them the path. Ethel wished they

---

[4] B/L, India Office Records L/Mil/15111: *Operations in Manipur, 1891.*
[5] *Ibid.*

could take his advice and thus avoid any more fighting, but the officers decided to push on, believing he was not telling the truth.

They had scarcely gone half a mile when they saw a stockade blocking the road and decided to rush it. Ethel, fearing its sharp bamboos would rip her skirt, turned away, and in doing so stumbled into a deep ditch. They were being fired on by the enemy and were returning their shots, but it was difficult to see where the marksmen were, as they were screened by the trees around them.

Suddenly there was a shout that men were coming up the hill—they were a long way off, so it was impossible to see whether they were friend or foe. After what seemed to Ethel an eternity it was discovered that they were Captain Cowley's men. They were saved! Urged to make one last effort, and helped by the officers, she joined in the rush down the hill to meet them. With 'a mist in her eyes and surging head,' she 'ran as [she] had never run before'[6] until she tripped over a large stone and twisted her ankle. Sick and giddy with pain, she sat down at the edge of the road and sobbed, for the strain had been more than she could bear. Tears came as a relief after the horrors of the past days.

Cowley had started for Imphal with sixteen elephants and seventeen ponies, but carried rations for only ten days, having expected to get fresh supplies on arrival. Before coming across the fugitives he and his men had had a difficult march through heavy rain, slippery mud and the swollen Jhiri river. They had been surprised as they neared Leimatak to be shot at, and could only guess that there had been trouble at Imphal. Early the next day they heard the bugle call of the 42nd Gurkhas on the hill above them. Cowley, suspecting a trap, advanced to reconnoitre, and found some sepoys who informed him that there had been a disaster at Manipur, and that some fugitives, with a lady, were in the jungle on top of a ridge about six miles away, so he and his troops marched on to their rescue.

Although Ethel's party was saved, they were still in enemy territory, so after a rest and a share of Cowley's men's rations of potted meat, biscuits, soda water and whisky, they moved off.

---

[6] *My Three Years*, Grimwood.

Ethel's ankle was so painful that for the first part of the journey she had to be carried in a dhooly, but was later able to support it with a woollen stocking inside a sepoy's large boot.

Cowley took the initiative of asking Boileau, who was officially his senior but exhausted, permission to take command. Having done so, he sent Gurdon on ahead, ordering him to double march to Cachar to report what had happened. He had made the decision to return to Cachar with the fugitives and obtain fresh troops and supplies before advancing to the aid of the prisoners in the palace.

That evening they reached Leimatak, where they halted, ate and slept. By this time they had been joined by as many as 175 fleeing men and their followers and had another five days' march ahead before they could re-cross the Jhiri river and reach the safety of the frontier. Ethel wrote:

> Our march was very monotonous. We got up at three every morning and marched until sunset. We had a meal of army rations and cocoa in the morning, and another in the evening, after which we all went to sleep as we were, and never woke up until the bugle sounded the reveille. We were always dead-tired. The hills were very steep and ... the heat intense during the day, and the cold piercing at night. We could only move very slowly, and with caution, for we never knew when we might be attacked.[7]

They were not attacked, however, for the Manipuris found them too large a party to tackle, but they were sporadically fired at. This, Ethel found, made her far more nervous than when she had been in imminent danger. As they marched they set fire to the thanas in their path, finding several baskets of rice in one before they did so. This eased the problem of feeding the sepoys and their large number of followers, who had had to be put on half rations.

On 1 April they reached Lahkipur and the safety of British territory at last. Here Ethel was able to change into clean clothes sent from Cachar, and have a proper breakfast, which seemed a complete luxury. It was from here that she sat down the following

---

[7] *My Three Years*, Grimwood.

day to write her sister-in-law, Mabel, a very long and detailed account of all that had happened, ending:

> ...You being a woman can understand what I had to go through in addition to all this, with a lot of men utter strangers to me, but they were kindness itself as far as they could be. Now it remains to be seen what is to be done about getting back the prisoners, and my anxiety on this account I can't express. People say they will all be safe, but until I see Frank again I shall not be content ... it is simply awful living in suspense like this, and I almost wish I were a prisoner too....[8]

In the early hours of the next morning, Ethel and the men resumed their march to cover the last fourteen miles to Cachar. She arrived to find herself greeted as a heroine.

---

[8] RA VIC/N/47/175. By permission of Queen Elizabeth II.

5

Headline News

Rumours of the disaster at Manipur began to be spread by traders who had fled Imphal at the onset of fighting. Gurdon, who had been sent ahead with despatches to General Collett, the officer commanding Assam, arrived on British territory on 31 March with the first accurate account of what had happened. This was forwarded to the government of India, and met with incredulity. How could crack Ghurka forces, belonging to the finest regiments of the Bengal army, have been routed by the rude militia of an unwarlike people? The India Office in Whitehall, informed by telegram, judged the situation 'quite incomprehensible'. 'Troops,' they noted, 'seem to have been placed at a great disadvantage, and apparently the officers in command were not aware of the preparations being made for opposition.'[1]

The first intimation that there had been a disaster was published in *The Times* on Tuesday, 31 March—a week after the event. Its information was confused, and came from two fugitive Gurkhas of the Assam frontier police who had reached Kohima, and two guards who had been stationed at Langthabal, near Manipur, and had escaped to Tammu, 64 miles away on the Burmese border. They did not know what had happened to Quinton's party, only that Lieutenant Brackenbury was dead. *The Times* reported with irony that the guns used against the Residency had been those presented by the British Government to the late Maharajah. The news the next day, 1 April, was still confused, although the murder of poor Melville, the telegraph officer,

---

[1] B/L, India Office Records L/Mil/7/15106: *Operations in Manipur, 1891.*

was confirmed. He had been hindered by his crippled leg in trying to escape, and had been beheaded while in hiding and asleep.

As soon as the report of the disaster reached the Viceroy, Lord Lansdowne, he cancelled an intended tour and summoned the Council to meet him in haste at Simla, the summer capital. Immediately a massive invasion force was ordered to advance on Manipur in three columns from the north, south and east, their object being to release the prisoners, and then take Imphal.

Relatives in England, meanwhile, waited anxiously for news. Winchester College, Frank's old school, had received a telegram telling of the critical situation he was in, and both staff and boys had gathered to pray for him in chapel. The British found it hard to acknowledge that the rebellion had gone against them.

On 2 April the news was reported of the safe arrival of Ethel, Boileau, Butcher, Woods, Lugard and Calvert. At the same time, *The Times* also published an account of an interview that the ex-Maharajah of Manipur had given a Calcutta newspaper, in which he blamed the Senapati for his overthrow, and Grimwood and Quinton for having been fooled and deceived by him.

The Manipur disaster now occupied the pages of *The Times* to the extent that news of it dwarfed all other topics during the week. 'The public is now awaiting news of the prisoners with intense anxiety' it proclaimed. '... It cannot be denied that their position is one of grave peril, [but] the general impression is that their captors will attempt no further violence, in the hope of thereby securing for themselves better terms.'[2]

Major General Sir James Johnstone, ex-Political Officer in Manipur and author of *My Experiences in Manipur*, wrote a succession of letters to *The Times* over the course of the next few months. He had never liked the Senapati, whom he described as 'cruel, coarse and low-minded'.[3] Johnstone felt that the instant the Regent refused to have the Senapati arrested a force should have entered the palace and captured the guns and magazine. As it was, the delay had made the Senapati more confident, and when the

---

[2] *The Times*, 6 April 1891, p.5.
[3] *My Experiences in Manipur and the Naga Hills*, Sir James Johnstone, 1896.

troops did enter the palace, the capture of the guns had not appeared to be their first object. The retreat was a fatal mistake, for 'he who retreats before an Asiatic is doomed'.[4] Johnstone pointed out that the problem over the lack of ammunition had been another factor, due to the incompatibility between the arms carried by Quinton's escort and those of the Residency guard.

While England waited breathlessly for news, Ethel, who was staying with friends in Cachar, was finding it

> delightful to have a woman to talk to again, although my companions on the march had one and all shown me how unselfish and kindhearted Englishmen can be when they are put to the test. They had never let me feel that I was a burden on them, and though often I felt very weak and cowardly, they quieted my misgivings, and praised me for anything I did, so that it gave me courage to go on and help to endure the horrors of that terrible retreat.[5]

Despite the kindness of the friends she was staying with, Ethel was increasingly tormented by anxiety for her husband, although the general opinion was that he and the rest of the party were safe with their captors. In her misgivings she remembered stories of the Indian Mutiny, and how prisoners had been murdered just at the moment rescue was imminent. She must also have thought of her father's elder brother, William, a magistrate at Mirzapore, who had been one of those killed. In desperation, Ethel wrote two letters to her husband telling him of her own escape and ordeal, and addressed them to the Regent. The only condition made on her writing them was that she said nothing of the preparations being made to rescue the prisoners, for Cachar was now alive with military activity.

Ethel had been in Cachar one week when she saw a telegram from Shillong delivered to the Deputy Commissioner's bungalow, while she was visiting there with her hostess. As it was handed over she remarked that she disliked bright yellow envelopes, for

---

[4] *My Experiences in Manipur*, Johnstone.
[5] *My Three Years in Manipur*, Ethel Grimwood, 1891.

12 Ethel St. Clair Grimwood. *(Illustrated London News Picture Library)*

they always meant bad news—then noticed how upset the Commissioner looked.

Her hostess broke the news to her as soon as they reached home: Frank, Quinton and their entire party had been murdered.

Ethel was so stunned that she spent several hours trying to persuade herself that the news was not true—there must have been a mistake. The cruel confirmation came, however, the

13 Frank Grimwood, Political Agent at Manipur. *(Illustrated London News Picture Library)*

following morning in a letter from Kulachandra, the Regent. This at first implied that Frank had been killed in the fighting, but later made clear that the party had been murdered on the orders of the Senapati.

Directly he heard the news of the trouble in Manipur, Lieutenant Charles Grant, of the 2nd battalion, 4th Gurkhas, whom

Ethel and Frank had enjoyed meeting at Tammu in Burma, and with whom Ethel had made and burnt a cake, requested permission to go to the relief of the captives. His dash and pluck in guerilla warfare had already attracted attention, and much hope was laid on him. Taking eighty Gurkhas and Punjabis, together with three elephants and a few ponies and coolies, he set off for Imphal, fighting his way there with great daring and courage. Only twenty of his troops were seasoned old soldiers; the rest were recruits who had only fired a few rounds at musketry practice. Another hazard was that their road was made almost impassable by being strewn with cut and twisted telegraph wires, and further blocked by trees which had been felled across it.

While on his way, Grant heard that the Sahibs had been killed but that the Memsahib and a few officers had escaped. He sent the news to Captain Presgrave of the 12th Burma Infantry who was due to relieve him at Tammu, telling him of his own position and what he intended to do.

Three days after their start, Grant's party reached Thobal, ten miles south of Imphal. It was early morning, and they crawled in relays towards the enemy compound, firing as they did so, having had to cross a river to reach it. Once over they found an enemy line over a mile long, so that their very small party was facing eight hundred troops. Grant was forced to decide that instead of pushing on to Manipur they would have to stay put and occupy the mud fort they had reached, which they hastily stocked with what rice, sugar-cane juice, green dhal, paddy and peas they could find.

The next morning Grant's patrols reported that the enemy were advancing in full force against them. They managed to hold them off in the morning, but from the afternoon onwards their position was shelled until dark, and the firing continued from long range during the night. The following afternoon a Gurkha appeared with a white flag to tell them that he was a prisoner of the Regent, and was one of about a hundred hostages who would be killed if Grant advanced, but released if he retired. Somewhat suspicious, Grant deceived him by pretending he was a General Howlett, with a full regiment at his back, and kept up an exchange of messages with the Regent and Senapati for the next five days, refusing to move unless the prisoners, especially the Gurkhas, were released. Finally a messenger came to tell them that the prisoners had been sent to Assam, and to offer them food if they would retire. Grant sent the man and his provisions back, refusing to move unless a member of the durbar was sent as a hostage.

One week later, on 6 April, Grant and his men were again attacked. By now his ammunition was running out, so he ordered his troops to lie low, hoping that if they did so the enemy would be enticed near enough to shoot. He reported afterwards that his men had been 'simply splendid'. They had refused no orders, and had paid the closest attention to them, even under the hottest fire 'being particularly steady under shell-fire'.[6] They were still holding their position after two days, when a messenger appeared with a white flag and letters from Captain Presgrave ordering them to retire.

Presgrave wrote that he could not reinforce Grant, but would cover his retreat. Reluctantly, therefore, at 7.30 p.m. that night, Grant and his men started to move back towards Tammu. It was pitch dark and raining, with occasional flashes of lightning, so that they could only make a mile an hour. Luckily the bad weather enabled them to pass through Manipuri villages without being challenged, so that by 2 a.m. they had joined up with Presgrave and his troops. The latter had marched thirty-six hours non-stop without rations to reach them, having heard that Grant's force had either been captured or killed.

Once more on the road, they found themselves again confronted by a large Manipuri force, but managed to rout them after a hard fight, in which Grant's horse, Clinker, was shot from underneath him when at full gallop 300 yards from the front line, forcing him to continue fighting on foot.

Once safely in camp, Grant commended all his men for an Order of Merit for their bravery in attack, siege and retreat. He himself was awarded the Victoria Cross for his 'conspicuous bravery and devotion to his country . . . (having) inspired his men

---

[6] *The Manipur Expedition* 1891, G.Couchman, 1891.

with equal heroism and an ever-present example of personal daring and resource'.[7] Telegrams of congratulations arrived from the Viceroy and General Roberts, Chief of Staff, and he was raised immediately to the rank of Major.

Despite being showered with praise, Grant was disgusted to find that he and his troops now had to wait for reinforcements before going into action again. At last on 25th April they received orders to march some seven miles due north on the plain towards Manipur, where a substantial enemy force was entrenched on an oval-shaped earthwork topped by a parapet with large hollow bamboos inserted as loopholes for guns. Unknown to the British, around three sides of the earthwork, completely concealed by grass, was a treacherous 'nullah' filled with water and with precipitous overhanging banks.

As Grant and Captain Drury advanced with their men across the open plain towards the earthwork it was being furiously shelled by Captain Rundall of the 4th Gurkhas from a small hill opposite, the Manipuris returning fire with jinjals[8]. On reaching the earthwork, Grant's troop joined with another under Captain Carnegy to attack the north, west and south faces simultaneously.

In his *Report* Captain Rundall wrote,

> Both Gurkhas and Sikhs were magnificently led by their officers and native officers, and advanced under heavy fire with the utmost steadiness and coolness. When sufficiently close they fixed bayonets and charged shoulder to shoulder, but were pulled up for a moment by the nullah, of whose existence they were unaware ... leaping down into it they endeavoured to find a way out of it. Owing to the difficult precipitous side they could only scramble out in knots. One of the enemy's men stood opposite to Captain Drury and held up a cleft stick with a piece of white paper inserted into it. Taking this for a flag of truce Capt. Drury held up his hand to stop his men, who began to cease firing. The man seeing this laughed and fired....[9]

---

[7] *The Victoria Cross 1856–1920* Sir O'More Creagh V.C. & E.M.Humphris, (eds) 1924.
[8] Indian swivel rifles.
[9] *The Manipur Expedition* G.H.H. Couchman

At this moment Grant 'felt a tremendous blow on the neck and staggered and fell, luckily on the edge of the ditch, rather under cover, but feeling the wound with my finger, and being able to speak, and feeling no violent flow of blood, I discovered I wasn't dead just yet. So I reloaded my revolver and got up.'[10] He later found that a bullet had gone right through the root of his neck, just above the shoulder, and had carried some of the cloth of his collar and shirt right through the wound, though leaving it quite clean. He continued fighting, killing a great many of the enemy.

The waving of the paper was probably a piece of individual treachery as no flag of truce was shown elsewhere. Rundall's *Report* continues, 'Directly ... officers and men saw the treachery they rushed into the work ... even when our men got in the enemy would not give way, some firing out of the ditches and shelter trenches, others with clubbed muskets and swords furiously resisted, and both sides engaged in a desperate hand to hand fight which, however, did not last long, as the enemy could not withstand the determined onslaught of our officers and men, who with swords, bayonets and kukris cut them down in heaps. ...'[11] This was the famous Battle of Khongjom, in which some 400 Manipuris died for their country in a last desperate bid to save its independence from British rule.

On 19 April Brigadier General Collett had issued a proclamation from Kohima:

> As the British Government and its forces have been opposed by the armed forces of Manipur state that state has become guilty of open rebellion against H.M. Queen Empress of India. The authority of the Regent, Kula Chandra Dhuja Singh is therefore declared to be at an end, and until the further pleasure of the British Government is known I shall exercise supreme authority over the state. Further the people of Manipur are warned against resisting my advance. I am going to Manipur to take possession of the capital and to punish, as they deserve, all who have acted as leaders or instigators of the revolt or who have been concerned in the treacherous murder of British subjects.[12]

---

[10] *My Three Years in Manipur*, Ethel Grimwood
[11] Ibid.
[12] *Queen Empress v. Tikendrajit*, John Parratt, 1992.

14 Lieutenant Grant, who was wounded in the famous battle of Khongjom, and won a V.C. for his bravery, being carried back to Tammu. *(Illustrated London News Picture Library)*

As soon as news of the disaster had reached the Viceroy, three very large columns of troops had been ordered to advance on Manipur: 1,000 men under General Collett from Kohima, 1,600 rifles under Colonel Rennick from Cachar, and Grant and Presgrave's column, commanded by General Graham. By coincidence all three forces entered Imphal on the same day, 27 April, having had a slow and difficult march through rain, mud and difficult terrain to get there, particularly those coming from Cachar. They entered the town in pouring rain, and found it completely deserted and abandoned. The royal family and army had fled, fearing the massive columns of men marching on them, leaving the palace in shambles. The Residency itself had been burnt and every brick thrown down. Even the shrubs in the garden had been rooted up, and the graves disturbed, including that of the small son of General Johnstone, who had died at the Residency. The bodies of two of the murdered men had been buried in Heath's grave, while the others were discovered outside in the polo ground. The heads of all of them had been severed and buried separately in a small, brick-lined hole.

Some of the troops were billeted in the palace buildings, while Collett blew up other buildings, including the dragons[13] in front of which Quinton's party had been executed. The bodies of the dead were exhumed in the presence of a committee which included Captain Boileau and Dr Calvert, but were so mutilated and decomposed that identification was difficult. Lieutenant Colonel St. John Michell, one of those who had had the job of finding and identifying them, described it as 'the most dreadful task I ever had to do'.[14] Even Frank's brother, Major Grimwood, could not positively identify Frank's body. The *Pioneer*'s correspondent wrote:

> Those who are preaching mercy, and maundering about the consideration due to the Native States, should have been here when the bodies were

---

[13] The statues had dragons' heads and lions' feet. They may have been representative of the ouroboros, a mythological serpent with its tail in its mouth symbolising eternity, popular in Manipur.

[14] N/A PRO 30/40/12/3: Miscellaneous papers including the Grimwoods and Manipur, 1888–1892.

exhumed, and the painful task of identification was sorrowfully gone through. They would then perhaps have realised to the full extent how treacherously the lives of five British officers were taken, and how helpless we now are in the matter of inflicting punishment upon those who connived at, and even instigated the massacre.[15]

The burial took place with full military honours, Frank's brother being among the chief mourners. A cortège made up by one company from each of the regiments in Imphal marched along the street lined with Gurkhas to the cemetery, which was near the Residency, to the sound of guns fired at one-minute intervals. As General Collett read the funeral service over the bodies, the King's Royal Rifles fired three volleys over the graves, and the murdered officers were laid to rest.

Gradually the story of the murders was pieced together from accounts given by native witnesses, but not before the press had had a field day spreading lurid descriptions of the 'revolting barbarity'[16] of them. They reported that the mutilated bodies had been thrown over the city walls to the pariah dogs, and their blood sprinkled over the mouths of the carved dragons which stood in front of the royal palace.

It will never be known what exactly happened when Quinton and his party entered the palace gates. Their original intention had been to meet the Senapati midway between the gates and the Residency. Why, it was questioned, with the Residency no longer tenable and the Manipuris evidently in overwhelming force, were they induced to go in? They were not met by the Senapati at the gates as they expected, but by lesser palace officials, who invited them into the durbar room. There they were asked to consent to their troops laying down arms, which they refused to do. It seems that Quinton, now realising the danger they were in, tore a leaf from his pocket book and wrote, 'We are in a trap, they want us to make over our arms.' He gave it to one of the guards to deliver, but it never reached the Residency. All negotiations having failed, and no terms having been settled, Quinton turned to leave, and

---

[15] Compilation from the *Pioneer* newspaper, 1891.
[16] *The Times*, 13 April 1891, p. 5.

15 The Palace enclosure at Manipur: the scene of Frank Grimwood's murder. *(Illustrated London News Picture Library)*

the Senapati asked one of his officers to see the party out. As they reached the dragons on the steps they began to be hustled, and the outer gates were slammed in their faces. This inflamed the watching mob, who shouted, 'Kill them.'[17] The Manipuri guard, unable to calm them, began to push their way back to the durbar room followed by Quinton's party. Just as they were doing so, Simpson was struck a sharp blow on the head, and fell. Frank, who was in the rear, was then savagely speared by a Burmese knife or 'dhao' in the back, and died immediately. The Senapati afterwards claimed that when this happened he came down from the 'top guard',[18] beat off the attackers with a stick, and carried Simpson into the durbar hall himself, but had left Grimwood's body, knowing that if he touched it he would have to perform the atonement ceremony. He had assured the English that they should go back to the Residency as soon as the people had

---

[17] *Documents on Anglo-Manipur War 1891*, N. Khelchandra Singh, 1984.
[18] 'Top guard': a room in the palace.

become calm. Quinton, Skene, Cossins and Simpson were then imprisoned in the durbar room for two hours while their captors debated their fate. They were then put in irons, their legs chained and their hands tied behind their backs. This done, they were taken out into the moonlight and, watched by a large crowd, beheaded by a stroke from the dhao. Simpson, who had recovered consciousness, was among them, but so weak that he had had to be supported to his fate.

There were many conflicting statements about what happened in the palace during the two hours the prisoners awaited their fate. From all accounts it appears there was an argument between the Senapati and the Thangal General as to what to do with them. The Senapati afterwards claimed that it was the Thangal who had decided on their murder, while he himself returned to the top guard. He had been told of the decision and, taken by surprise, had said, 'This cannot be, let us go to the old man and confer.'[19] He then went to the Thangal and asked, 'Did you give the order to kill the officers?' The answer being in the affirmative, he had urged the impropriety of killing such high officers. The General had turned on him, saying, 'Have you lost your senses? Do you think there is any chance of reviving lost friendship with the British? It is better, therefore, to do away with them.'[20] In the Thangal General's eyes, the British had waged war against Manipur, and therefore, according to Manipuri law, they were punishable by death.

The Senapati claimed that after this argument with the Thangal he had gone to rest on his bed and, sick and exhausted through the fatigue of the day, had fallen asleep. Later the state executioner was to say that he had received his orders from both the Thangal *and* the Senapati. The day after the executions both the Regent and the Senapati were reported to have taken part in a street procession amid general rejoicing.

---

[19] *Queen Empress v. Tikendrajit*, Parratt.
[20] *Ibid.*

16 Lieutenant Walter Simpson, 43rd Gurkhas, friend of the Grimwoods, who was among those murdered on March 24, 1891. *(Illustrated London News Picture Library)*

6

A National Heroine

Immediately after Ethel and the other fugitives arrived in Cachar, Lieutenant Colonel St. John Michell, General Graham's Adjutant General, came to interview them. He heard accounts of what had happened from each officer in private, together with evidence given him by the sepoys and Manipuris. As will appear later, he seems to have been surprisingly antagonistic to Ethel, and disinclined to believe her evidence, taking no account of the fact that she must have been in a state of deep shock.

After two weeks with her friends in Cachar, Ethel made her way to Calcutta, where she stayed with a Mr Apcar and started to try to piece together her shattered life, buying clothes and arranging her passage home. It is said she was accompanied on the voyage by her half-brother, Captain Boisragon.

Ethel arrived back in England at the beginning of June 1891 to find herself a national heroine, for not only had Manipur been headline news since the disaster broke, but the current state of affairs was continuing to be reported in the press daily. The *Illustrated London News* was also publishing a spectacular weekly article on the affair. These continued until August, and were superbly and very accurately illustrated.

Although she may have enjoyed her new-found fame, Ethel must have been very aware of the controversy raging over the disaster, and the distressing questions being asked about her husband's role in it, with the insinuation that he had been weak and inexperienced. The press questioned whether he should have reinstated the Maharajah by force, or perhaps have appointed his son in his stead, rather than let the Senapati's faction get their way. Quinton, too, had come under increasing criticism for having planned to arrest the Senapati in what seemed to the general public a deceitful and underhand way. Had the plan been his own, or had it originated from the government of India? No one seemed to know. And why, it was asked, had he permitted *all* the senior officers to leave together for the palace with him? A friend of Quinton, the Marquis of Ripon, had sprung to his defence in the House of Lords on 24 April, saying he had 'had much to do with him in the transaction of business, and always found him a man of marked ability, sound judgement and great moderation of character'.[1] It was because of the high esteem in which he was held that he had been appointed to the difficult post of Chief Commissioner of Assam the previous year.

While Ethel had been travelling home, a Military Court of Enquiry had been sitting in Imphal, where it was set up just three days after the British reoccupation. The Enquiry, a less stringent procedure than a Court Martial, was headed by a Colonel Evans, assisted by Major Eaton Travers (Gurkhas) and Captain A. Birch (Royal Artillery). It considered four areas of debate: a) the decision to withdraw from the residency; b) the manner of the withdrawal; c) the discipline of the troops on the march; and d) the fact that Cowley had returned to Cachar with Boileau's party rather than go directly on to Imphal to try to rescue the prisoners. All those who had escaped from Imphal were closely questioned, including several native troops. Ethel's written testimonies, prepared before she left India, were submitted to the court.

Boileau was the first witness to be called, having been the senior officer left at the Residency. He had already submitted his official report after his escape at the beginning of April, and it had raised embarrassing issues for the Viceroy, the government of India and the India Office. For although it was acknowledged that Quinton had made several mistakes, it was not felt to be in the interest of the government of India to publicly lay blame on its senior civil and military officers for lack of proper planning, poor intelligence or underestimating the strength and determination of the enemy,

---

[1] *The Times*, 25 April 1891, p. 8, col. A.

particularly now that they were dead. On the other hand, scapegoats had to be found, and sadly the blame was put on those junior officers who were still alive. The evidence that Boileau and his fellow officers gave at the trial varied, and there must have been a strong temptation to cover up.

Boileau was examined for three days, and charged with 'making no attempt to muster the men when at 1 a.m. on 25th March it was decided to retreat, so that nearly two thirds of the men were left behind, without orders from their officers'.[2] It was also alleged that he had 'behaved in an unsoldierlike manner in abandoning the Residency without observing established rules for conducting a retreat, that he did not parade his men or detail advance and rearguards before retreating, that he personally left before the evacuation was complete, and that on ascertaining that a large number of men had remained behind took no measures to communicate with them but left them to their fate'. Lastly, he was accused of 'failing to maintain order and discipline in retreat and allowing the retreating party to straggle and separate in a perilous and unsoldierlike manner'.[3]

In his defence, Boileau stated that he was not aware of leaving any troops behind, believing them to be with Lieutenant Chatterton. However, Chatterton, who was Skene's staff officer, and described as a 'most important witness', for whom the trial had been held up while he was summoned back from Dibrughar to give evidence, made two damaging points. First, when the ceasefire ended, he had called Boileau, who was making the rounds of the men at their posts, back to the house, as the rest of the officers now felt it imperative to retire. Boileau, however, instead of giving the lead, had said he would 'abide by the decision of the majority'.[4] The second point was the fact that after the escape he had found Boileau and Butcher standing in the road about one mile from the Residency. On reporting that there were still men to wait for, Boileau had replied this could only be done when they got out

---

[2] N/A WO 32/8400: *Proceedings of Court of Enquiry into events of March 1891, at Manipur.*
[3] *Ibid.*
[4] *Ibid.*

into the open country about half a mile away, the place they were standing in being thick with houses. When they got to the open, however, any question of waiting was dropped, despite the fact that Boileau only had about a third of his men with him.

Major-General Galbraith, Adjutant General to the Military Secretary in India, summing up the court's findings, wrote that Boileau 'had shown himself unequal to the emergency in which he was placed'.[5]

Captain Butcher was the second witness to be called, the charges against him being:

1 & 2) He had omitted to take any effective steps on the afternoon of 24 March to recall Lieutenant Simpson's party, or to assure himself of Surgeon Calvert's whereabouts before he left the Jubraj's temple to return to the Residency.
3) When the retreat from the Residency had been decided on he failed to collect the men of his battalion in order that the retreat might be conducted in a proper and soldierlike manner. He never left the Residency to check on his men lining the compound walls.
4) He personally left the Residency before evacuation was complete.
5) He failed to offer Captain Boileau any support or counsel.
6) He took no measures to communicate with the men left behind in the compound.
7) He failed to maintain discipline in his detachment during the retreat.

In his defence, Butcher replied that he had been deadbeat by the evening of the 24th, having been active from 4.30 a.m. He had finally fallen asleep, but had awoken at midnight when a shell struck the Residency and it was again under heavy fire. He had taken no steps to count the men before leaving, it being impossible on account of the darkness of the night—though other

---

[5] N/A WO 32/8400 *Proceedings of Court of Enquiry.*

witnesses recorded that it was bright moonlight. He had not returned to the compound because of the difficulty of retracing his steps through the villages, and there was a severe shortage of ammunition.

The questioning of the other witnesses, such as the surgeon, Calvert, was carried out in the same vein, each of them tending to point out small inaccuracies in what had been said. Captain Cowley, who was accused of returning to Cachar after rescuing the fleeing party rather than going on to Manipur to try and rescue the prisoners, said in his defence that any attack by him would probably have been the signal for their massacre, and that he had no rations beyond those for the next day. He had felt it inadvisable to leave the party of fugitives, who were in an exhausted state, to find their own way to safety.

The 27th witness, who was examined for a second time on 25 May, the last day of the trial, was Lieutenant Williams of the 43rd Gurkha Rifles, who handed over the two letters that Ethel had written him about the expected arrival of Quinton, and how they sensed it would lead to trouble.

The Military Enquiry was very little reported in the press, and Boileau later claimed that it was cloaked in secrecy. This is borne out by a communication from the Government of India Military Department to Viscount Cross at the India Office:

> We do not consider that it is desirable, in the interests of the army and of the state, that these proceedings should be published, containing as they do revelations as to the conduct of British officers which have made disciplinary actions necessary ... this would be in harmony with the procedure adopted in regard to military courts of enquiry generally, which the Secretary of State for War has always refused to produce to parliament.[6]

The report following the trial suggested that Boileau be suspended from active duty, his state of health demanding an immediate change of climate. He had, it was said, shown want of ability and judgement rather than neglect of duty. However, the

---

[6] *Queen Empress v. Tikendrajit*, Parratt.

final decision as to his future and that of the others would only be made in six months' time. Therefore, Boileau and Butcher were subjected to a long wait before knowing what the future held for them. In the event, Boileau was compulsorily retired from the service with a compassionate allowance of £200 per annum rather than the normal £250. He returned to England and became an army tutor until the outbreak of war in 1914, when he was re-employed as a recruiting officer at Cranbrook, Kent. A year later, having reached retirement age, he started to work for the Army Scripture Readers and Soldiers' Friend Society. Finding himself short of funds for supporting his wife, three daughters and third son (who was still a pupil at Dulwich), he applied for an addition to his pension, but was refused. As late as 1962 his son, Colonel Digby Boileau, wrote, 'there is in my opinion good reason to think that my father was victimised; that he was made a scapegoat for those really responsible, and sacrificed to public opinion chagrined at the loss of British prestige ... there is a cloak of secrecy over the business'.[7]

The judgement on Butcher was equally severe, the Viceroy writing the following to Viscount Cross in Whitehall on 25 August: 'His conduct showed an unsoldierly disregard for the welfare of his men and such neglect of the duties manifestly imposed on him by the situation of affairs, that his retention in H.M. Army is undesirable and we accordingly recommend his compulsory removal from the service.'[8] Having served twelve years, he was retired on a pension of 5 shillings a day.

Butcher, unlike Boileau, did not take his dismissal lying down, responding by demanding that he be given the 'N.E. Frontier clasp', awarded for the 1891 Manipur expedition. As this request had no precedent, his application had to go for personal approval by the Queen, who turned it down. On 25 January 1892 he wrote a long letter to the India Office in defence of all points made against him. Meeting with no success, he tried again on 30 April, writing

---

[7] B/L, India Office Records L/Mil/7/15114: *Proceedings of Court of Enquiry into occurrences of March 1891 at Manipur.*
[8] *Ibid.*

in a large flourishing hand to the Under Secretary of State, India Office with the request that he either be tried by court martial or at least granted a Court of Enquiry, as he wished to have the opportunity of defending himself against the seven charges preferred against him, which he was confident of having the evidence to disprove. He wrote: 'I would submit that whereas the meanest of Her Majesty's subjects is permitted to defend himself in Court against any charge, however trivial, I have not been allowed to refute in Court the accusations brought against me, nor of ever hearing the evidence, which in any case is unsworn.'[9] Butcher's repeated requests for a review were all turned down. No court martial ever took place, and the findings of the Court of Enquiry were never published.

The Government of India now had to decide what the future of Manipur should be. Some felt that annexation was the only way to punish the people and restore British prestige. This would also have the advantage of allowing better communications between Upper Burma and Assam, and provide a stronghold from which to subdue the turbulent local tribes. The position was left unresolved until the autumn, but meanwhile there was trouble over the appointment of a new Political Officer. A Mr McCabe had been chosen, but almost unbelievably, before taking up his position, was found by Colonel Rennick to be a drunkard on the verge of madness. Instead, Major St. John Maxwell, Deputy Commissioner at Cachar, was given the post. He went on to have a long association with the state, and did much that was good for Manipur, doubtless aided by his Manipuri mistress, Princess Sanatombi, who, by a strange twist of fate, was the daughter of the deposed Maharajah. Their liaison, although childless, created a scandal, and led to their being lampooned in the popular rhymes of the day.

All this time an intensive hunt was going on to find the murderers of the British officers. On 4 May Mya Mynzarrow, the man thought to have speared Frank Grimwood, was captured and brought into Imphal on a litter, having been wounded in the

---

[9] B/L, India Office Records L/Mil/7/15114: *Proceedings of Court of Enquiry*.

fighting. A few days later Kulachandra the Regent was arrested, and the Thangal General gave himself up. The Senapati, who had a large price on his head, remained free. However, following the Indian police officers' maxim 'that the most certain way to capture an absconding native criminal is to watch his village',[10] he was found by two officers of the frontier police hiding with a relative about six miles from the palace. No one had believed he would allow himself to be taken alive, but he was overcome after a fierce struggle, having been weakened by being in hiding, and had to be carried to Imphal on a coolie's back. The Viceroy, Lord Lansdowne, was so pleased with the arrests that he sent a telegram to Major Maxwell congratulating him.

Landsdowne had been careful to keep the Queen informed of all the events of the disaster since the news first broke on 31 March. The Queen-Empress was at that time emotionally involved with India, for at her Golden Jubilee four years earlier she had acquired two Indian servants. These were the fat and smiling Mahomet and the slim and clever 24-year-old Abdul Karim. The latter had risen from waiting at table to being her 'Munshi' or teacher. She was taking a daily Hindi lesson after tea with him, as well as tuition in sociology and religion. She was fascinated by learning about a people with whom she had had no real contact before, and would hear no criticism of her teacher.

The Queen threw herself into the Manipur situation with passion, sending endless cypher telegrams to both the Viceroy and the Minister of State for India, Viscount Cross. For instance, on 6 April she telegraphed Cross from Grasse in France, saying, 'Fear from the Reuters report that the affair is becoming more serious which is very distressing. But it is only these wild hill tribes, I think. Our commissioners are not of the right kind: bumptious and not understanding how to deal with these people.'[11]

On hearing that the offer of a reward had been made for the capture of the murderers, the Queen became very concerned about what punishments should be meted out to them, and on 18

---

[10] *The Times*, 25 May 1891, p. 5, col. A.
[11] *Letters and Journals of Queen Victoria*, vol. 2, Esher & Buckle, (eds), 1907–1936.

A NATIONAL HEROINE

April telegraphed Lansdowne: 'While wish murderers if possible to be caught and duly punished, would earnestly deprecate any wholesale punishment for the incident or any incitement to bloody revenge. This, only too easily encouraged, would not redound to our honour or add to our power for the future.'[12]

This prompted Lansdowne to write to Sir Frederick Roberts, Commander-in-Chief in India, saying, '... it is just possible that the strong indignation which has been aroused in the public mind by the Manipur disaster may influence our troops and that there may be some difficulty in preventing them from resorting to inordinate reprisals ... it occurs to me, that you may possibly think well to give a private hint to the officers concerned that they and the troops must be extremely careful how they allow themselves to be carried away by their just indignation'.[13]

On the 2 May the Queen, who felt very maternal towards her Indian subjects, wrote,

> Our dealings in India should be dictated by straightforwardness, kindness and firmness, or we cannot succeed. This disaster is most unfortunate, and the effect may be very serious in other parts of India. Our system of sending out ... people who merely get appointed for passing an examination must be altered, or we shall have some much more serious trouble in India. There is no doubt, from what the Queen hears from many sides, that the natives (though they are very loyal to the Queen Empress and Royal Family) have no affection for the English rule, which is one of fear not love, and this will not answer for a conquered nation. One of the Royal family ought, if possible, to be constantly there to encourage the good feeling and loyalty of the people, which no private individual could in the same way, and certainly not people like many of those who are now in Indian employment.[14]

The Queen's scorn for those who passed the Indian Civil Service examinations was not entirely fair, for only about one out of four who took them was successful, competition being high because the post of Political Officer was well paid.

---

[12] *Letters and Journals of Queen Victoria*, Esher & Buckle.
[13] *Ibid.*
[14] *Ibid.*

Even after the trial the Queen continued to agitate about what she felt to be the inferiority of the Commissioners and Political Agents in India compared with former times. In response to her concern, the Viceroy wrote to say that Quinton, whom he had selected for the Chief Commissionership personally, was a gentleman much respected by all who knew him. He had served in India for 35 years, and had sat for a short time on his Legislative Council. He had been much liked, and would have been incapable of acting treacherously towards the Manipuri princes or anyone else. This sentiment would have been borne out by the Ilberts, with whom he had lodged for some time in Calcutta, and who were very fond of him, and thought him an engaging and congenial Irishman.

A special court was convened in June, as ordered by the Viceroy, to hear the cases against the Regent, the Senapati and other offenders, but it was difficult to find anybody qualified to conduct the trial. In the end, Lieutenant Colonel St. John Michell, who had examined the escaping party at Cachar, and who was well-experienced in this part of India, was appointed President. His assistants were Major Richard Ridgeway V.C. of the 44th Gurkha Rifles, a hero who had won his medal in the Naga Hills expedition of 1880 and had taken part in the recapture of Manipur, and A. W. Davis, Deputy Commissioner in Kohima.

Michell, who sounds to have been a difficult and possibly unbalanced character, wrote that 'the abominable trials were a perpetual anxiety' to him.[15] He was placed in a 'very unsatisfactory situation', having to use the civil code rather than have a Court Martial, which he would have much preferred. The man appointed to be his prosecutor had proved hopeless, so Maxwell, the new Political Agent, had had to take his place.

The Senapati, who was the first to be tried, was accused of waging war against the Queen, abetment of murder, and murder itself. All of these under British Indian law carried the death penalty or transportation for life. Early in the trial, Naik Kabinaj Thapa of 'E' company was called on to describe the attack on the

---

[15] N. Archives, PRO 30/40/12/3.

Senapati's house, which stood in a large walled and moated enclosure in the palace grounds, and the effort to arrest him. 'Arriving in front of the Senapati's house the sentry said he was not there,' he stated. 'Butcher asked where he had gone, as he had come to arrest him. Manipuri Subadar of household asked if Butcher had come to fight, set up a war cry. A gong sounded from palace in answer, a horn was blown, and fighting commenced to which we replied.' The Senapati had claimed in a telegram sent to the Viceroy on 9 April that 'my place was attacked on the early morning of the 24th—we were all asleep. Troops entered, killing sentries. The troops demolished our temple, sacred idols, killing women and children, set fire to houses, tied children by hair and threw them on fire . . .'[16] Lansdowne had accepted Boileau's report that the allegations were quite unfounded, although it was later agreed that Skene had been wrong to attack the Senapati's house in darkness, as his servants were bound to resist.

The Senapati further explained in his defence that the reason so many men were in the Palace was because they were required for parades; that he was unable to surrender himself owing to his being attacked; that he opened fire in his own defence; that he could not conduct the British officers to the gate as there was much firing going on at the time; that afterwards, being tired, he fell asleep and did not know that the officers were murdered until next morning; that when the men came asking him to confirm the Thangal General's order for the execution of the officers, he told them on no account to obey the order; and that he kept the officers because there were so many armed men about and he intended to release them in the morning. He admitted that he did not punish the Thangal General because he was 'an old and faithful servant, and great confusion prevailed'.[17] According to Sir James Johnstone, the Senapati had always been on bad terms with the Thangal General, and therefore it seems he did not hesitate to lay the blame for the murders on him, despite the fact that he was an old man of eighty-seven.

---

[16] B/L, India Office Records L/Mil 15106: *Operations in Manipur, 1891*.
[17] B/L, India Office Records L/Mil 7/15114: *Operations in Manipur, 1891*.

One of the key witnesses to appear against the Senapati was Captain Butcher, who claimed that during the retreat from the Residency he had seen messengers leave the palace and communicate with the villages lying ahead of them, inciting the villagers to fire on them.

When the time came to sum up, Michell failed to agree with the other two men on his commission, and it was only after two days' argument that judgement was reached, with that on the Senapati being passed on 14 June. He was found guilty of waging war against the Queen and of abetment of murder; in that he could have saved the officers, but had made no move to do so. He was, however, *not* found guilty of murder, not having been present at the executions. This had been the sticking point with Michell, who had felt that any leniency could encourage the murder of other Political Officers. In the end both the Senapati and the Thangal General were sentenced to death. There was a delay in confirming the sentences, as the mass of papers dealing with the court's proceedings had to be sent up to Simla, the post there from Manipur taking fourteen days. During this interval the prisoners were held in Imphal, and given access to a lawyer to frame their appeals. A clever senior member of the Calcutta bar, Mano Mohan Ghose, was engaged to act on their behalf, but they were refused permission to have their appeals heard in court, only being allowed written representation. Ghose argued that since Manipur was an independent state, none of those on trial were British subjects, and should, therefore, not be governed by the municipal laws of British India or tried by a British court. Furthermore, as none of the officers of the court had any legal training at all the prisoners had not been legally tried either under British law *or* the Indian Penal Code.

Ghose later wrote a book, *Did the Manipur Princes Obtain a Fair Trial?* in which he explained that the accused were not allowed the assistance of Counsel during their trial. In the Senapati's case his statement had been taken down by Babu Janoki Nath Bysak, a Manipuri trader with only a smattering of English, which the Special Correspondent of *The Pioneer* had corrected. A telegram had been sent to Ethel asking in what state of health

Frank had found the Senapati in the eve of the disaster, and she had replied 'Mr. Grimwood found Jubraj ill on evening 23 March'.[18]

Ghose concluded the appeal by arguing that the Princes had been effectively undefended, and therefore had not had a fair trial.

The delay in ratifying the sentences allowed Ghose to release sensational rumours and highly coloured telegrams about the English to the press. Prince Bhairabjit Singh (the Pucca Sena) also entered into the fray, writing Sir Mortimer Durand (Secretary to the Government of India) a scurrilous letter, now in the National Archives, in which he repeated the scandalous stories about the Grimwoods. He wrote how Frank, in Ethel's absence, and aided by the Senapati, had invited the nautch girls to come one by one to the Residency, to be photographed. Their parents had objected, on the grounds that it would make them unacceptable for marriage, and he himself had personally begged Grimwood to desist, saying that if he invited girls to the Residency (as he insinuated his predecessors, Dr Brown, Major Trotter and Mr Primrose had also done), he should at least be discreet about it. Frank had assured him that the visits had been merely for the purpose of photography, and had given his word that they would stop. However, shortly afterwards he had been seen rowing and amusing the girls in the tank in the Residency compound in company with the Senapati. Ethel, too, was accused of using her visit to Shillong and acquaintance with English 'gentlemen' to get favours for her husband. She was further accused of being on intimate terms with Captain Butcher on the retreat, and of having slept under the same blanket, 'to the scandal of the party'.[19] The mothers and sisters of the princes also wrote to the government, accusing Frank of having been idle and lazy when a Political Officer.

The Times judged that it had been a mistake to try the prisoners under British law; charges should have been made under the Indian Penal Code. They argued that if the Manipuris were

---

[18] *Did the Manipur Princes Obtain a Fair Trial?* William Hutchison & Co., London 1891.
[19] N/A PRO, 30/40/12/3.

17 The Thangal General, Regent and Senapati at the time of their capture in 1891. *(Illustrated London News Picture Library)*

feudatories they were guilty of rebellion, and should be tried by martial law; but if they were independent belligerents they should be charged with an offence against the law of nations—namely, the murder of an ambassador under a flag of truce. 'The public are now anxiously awaiting the final order of the Government on these cases,' the paper wrote; 'the more rabid section of the native Press, which has been sedulously attempting throughout to distort every incident connected with Manipur to the discredit of the Indian Government and its officers, is now loudly impugning the impartiality of the Court and the fairness of the trials . . .'[20] There was some truth in these accusations, for in setting up the court the procedures of British law had not been followed, and none of those conducting the trial had any professional knowledge of legal matters. The prisoners were not represented by Counsel, and were cross-examined in a way wholly at variance with normal legal

---

[20] *The Times*, 22 June 1891, p. 5, col. A.

practice. It has also been suggested that the defendants may not have fully understood the questions which they were asked, and were made to sign statements in English which they probably did not understand, for although the trial was conducted in Manipuri, Urdu and English, only English was used in recording it.

After the trial the Queen continued to agitate about the quality of the Indian Civil Service, and became almost obsessed about the punishment to be meted out to the Senapati, the Thangal General, the Regent and other princes. On 16 June she telegraphed Viscount Cross from Balmoral, saying, 'Think hanging Senapati would never do; it would create very bad feeling in Manipur and in all India. But shut him up for life in some distant part. Think no prince was ever hung. The Tongal [Thangal] deserves to be hung.'[21]

---

[21] *Letters & Journals of Queen Victoria*, Vol. 2, Esher & Buckle (eds). The Thangal General is often referred to in records as the 'Tongal'.

7

Ethel and the Queen

While Ethel was still in India, the Queen had shown an interest in her, and the Viceroy had reported that 'Mrs. Grimwood was most deeply touched by your Majesty's thoughtful enquiries after her health'[1]. After her return, the Queen summoned her to an audience at Windsor Castle on 1 July, that evening recording the whole interview in her journal:

> After luncheon saw poor Mrs. Grimwood who escaped from Manipur, and has been back about a month. Lady Cross brought her in and presented her, leaving her with me afterwards. She is striking-looking, with a fine figure and a pretty, sad face, but looks much worn and weather-beaten. She was a little shy at first, but got over it by degrees, and answered all I asked her, telling me a great deal of what she went through, which really is more than any woman, and above all, a lady, has ever done! She was nine days on the horrible march, and almost all the time followed and pursued. She was lame from having fallen, when she ran the last stockade on leaving Manipur. There were 9 officers and 200 men, who however were reduced to 40 at the last. She was continually aimed at and had to lie down and hide in the long grass. She had no clothes but those she was wearing. Once she saw herself being aimed at, and the man close behind her, who was already wounded, was killed, knocking her over and covering her with blood. In this condition she had to go on her way. She was thankful that her poor husband was killed on the spot, speared she thinks by someone who might have owed him a grudge, and this she thinks may have led to the murder of the others.
>
> She knew the Senapati very well and liked him very much, as she did all the Princes, with whom she used to ride about a great deal. She said she could not, and would not, believe he intended to kill the prisoners. But

---

[1] *Letters & Journals of Queen Victoria*, vol.2, Esher & Buckle (eds), 1907–1936.

the Tongal, who commanded the troops, was a horrible blood-thirsty old man of eighty-six, who had killed no end of men, women and children when he went out to punish tribes. Poor Mrs. Grimwood has lost everything she ever possessed. She saw the destruction of her rooms and could not get in to save anything. She went down to the poor wounded, but that was not safe, so they tried to move them out, and in doing so poor Lieutenant Brackenbury died. He was quite young and had fifteen bullets in him. The noise of the incessant firing was fearful. The whole haunted her like a nightmare; she still cannot sleep or bear to be alone. She was a good deal overcome once or twice in speaking. I gave her the Royal Red Cross, which pleased her very much, and pressed her hand and kissed her when she left. Poor thing, I pity her so much![2]

The Royal Red Cross had been instituted by the Queen on 27 April 1883, Florence Nightingale being an early recipient. It was the first military medal to be created solely for women, and was awarded to Ethel 'in recognition of her devotion to the wounded under most trying circumstances, during the attack on the Residency at Manipur'.[3] Ethel was afterwards painted and photographed wearing the badge, as directed, on her left shoulder; it was in the shape of a cross, enamelled red, edged with gold, with the words 'Faith, Hope, Charity 1883' engraved on the arms of the cross.[4]

That Ethel continued to speak so well of the Senapati to the Queen is fascinating considering all that had happened, and that his death sentence had been confirmed only the previous week. She seems to have formed such a strong attachment to him that she refused to believe he could be responsible for her husband's death, repeatedly saying that she could only remember the friendship he had shown them both. She may even have been in love with him, finding him a far more sympathetic person than the soldiers with whom she was surrounded, or even than her husband; someone with whom she could easily become intimate. She

---

[2] *Letters and Journals of Queen Victoria*, Esher & Buckle.
[3] *The Times*, 8 June 1891.
[4] The medal, which continues, is conferred on members of the nursing services irrespective of rank, and upon anyone, British or foreign, who has been recommended for special devotion or competency while engaged on hospital duties with the forces. It has now been divided into two classes, and is awarded to members of the nursing profession, both female and male.

18 Ethel photographed by Herbert Barraud in his studio at Oxford Street after her escape: she is wearing the Royal Red Cross awarded her personally by Queen Victoria. *(Hulton Archive, Getty Images Gallery)*.

failed to see the cruel side of his nature, which Major-General Sir James Johnstone emphasises in his book, *My Experiences in Manipur*.

A week before Ethel's audience with the Queen it had been announced that the Secretary of State for India, on the recommendation of the government of India, had awarded her a state pension of £140 per annum for life, to be paid quarterly.[5] This was equivalent to the grant normally made to the widow of a major killed in action; as a Chief Commissioner's widow, Mrs Quinton received a pension of £300 a year for life. Ethel was also given an additional special grant of £1,000 in consideration of 'the exceptional services rendered by her during the recent fighting in Manipur',[6] together with a further sum of £330 from the Bengal Civil Fund as compensation for her property destroyed in Manipur. Such was the sympathy for her that Princess Alexandra raised a subscription for her benefit from among the wives of officers, non-commissioned officers and men of the British army to honour her 'gallantry, heroism and devotion to the wounded under fire'.[7]

The Viceroy had had the report of the Military Court of Enquiry at Manipur in front of him by 30 June, together with the comments made on it by Sir Frederick Roberts, his powerful Commander-in-Chief. He wrote to the Queen that it was 'abundantly clear that there was grievous mismanagement', and that 'Colonel Skene seems never, even when the firing had begun, to have realised the position in which he was placed. The retreat was disorderly and discreditable, and there can be little doubt that, properly led, the force which remained was sufficient to hold its own even if the Residency was untenable ...'[8] In the same letter, which took three weeks to reach the Queen, Lansdowne grumbled about the civil servants in Whitehall and the government: 'The Viceroy cannot conceal from your Majesty that the tendency shown by the House of Commons to interfere with increasing

---

[5] IOL L/AG/21/6/22 No 253 in 'Army Widows Class C Pension Book Apr 1891–Mar 1895'.
[6] *The Times*, 24 June 1891, p. 9, col. D.
[7] *The Times*, 15 June 1891, p. 9.
[8] *Letters and Journals of Queen Victoria*, vol.2, Esher & Buckle (eds).

frequency in Indian affairs, with which it has at best a superficial acquaintance, greatly impairs the efficiency of the Government of India, and seriously affects the authority of your Majesty's representative ..."[9] He was obviously beginning to feel that the telegraph would soon reduce the great position he held to that of a puppet of Whitehall.

That Lansdowne had the double title of Governor-General and Viceroy went back to the days when India was run under the East India Company by a Governor-General. When the British government took over in 1858 after the mutiny the title was doubled with 'Viceroy'. The Viceroy governed with his council, and reported back to the Secretary of State for India, who had a seat in the cabinet.

Henry, 5th Marquis of Lansdowne, had become Viceroy in 1888 at the age of 43, following five years as Governor-General of Canada. He was a Liberal, and a great patrician and landowner, having large but indebted estates in England and Ireland, including palatial Bowood in Wiltshire and Lansdowne House in London. He was a slight, dapper man with a moustache, side-whiskers, and piercing, twinkling eyes. His polished manner was said to be inherited from his mother, who was the daughter of the Comte de Flahaut, Tallyrand's natural son. Lansdowne had a natural elegance, as can be seen in his letters to the Queen. He was not particularly engaged with India, but despite this he had tried to introduce certain reforms, such as curbing seditious articles in the press, dispensing with juries in murder trials in Bengal, stabilising the rupee (which had fallen to half its value) and introducing import duties. When he found himself defeated on the last two measures, he had complained, 'There is an impression in this country that Her Majesty's Government will not allow us to do anything.'[10]

Behind Lansdowne's patrician aura he was basically a simple, straightforward man, who relied on his salary as Viceroy to maintain his lands. He was naturally reticent, and disinclined to

---

[9] *Letters and Journals of Queen Victoria*, Esher & Buckle.
[10] *The Viceroys of India*, Mark Bence-Jones, 1982.

interfere with officials, which probably accounts for his government's laissez-faire attitude towards the overthrow of the Maharajah in Manipur. Despite this failing, he is thought to have dealt fairly with Manipur after the disaster, and to have had the courage to go ahead with the execution of the ringleaders, despite a reluctance to do so on the part of the British government and the Queen.

The Queen had evidently been much moved by Ethel's interview with her, and followed it up almost immediately with a letter written through her Lady in Waiting, Miss Ina McNeill, to which Ethel replied on 6 July, from 32 Eccleston Street, London:

> Thank you very much for your kind letter. I feel very greatly honoured that the Queen should take such a kind interest in me & shall lose no time in consulting Dr. Wharton Hood about my ankle. I have no copy of my letters relating to my experiences in Manipur by me just now, but I have written to my sister-in-law, Miss Grimwood for the letter I sent her, & as soon as I receive it I will make a copy of it & forward it to Her Majesty. It will be a very great pleasure to me to do so, & I am proud to think that the Queen desires to have the account.
>
> I shall be in London 'till the 18th July, when I go to Brighton on a visit to my Husband's Mother.
>
> I enjoyed my visit to Windsor very greatly, & can never express all I feel towards Her Majesty for the very great honour she has done me in permitting me to see her. It was far more than I expected or deserved— & it will always be a Red letter day to be remembered as long as I live.[11]

Once sentenced to death, the Senapati had appealed to Ethel by telegram, begging her to intercede on his behalf, which greatly distressed her. Perhaps influenced by Ethel's opinion of him, the Queen redoubled her efforts to have him spared. On 1 August she telegraphed Viscount Cross: 'Trust Senapati will not be executed. He was not found guilty of murder and the effect is sure to be bad in India! That harsh crushing policy will not do now. He should be shut up for life. There was too much that was not explained to make the case a clear one.'[12]

---

[11] RA VIC/N/47/174. By permission of Queen Elizabeth II.
[12] *Letters and Journals of Queen Victoria*, vol.2, Esher & Buckle (eds).

Cross, who was sympathetic to her feelings, replied on 9 August that he had written to the Viceroy 'so often and so strongly' that no prince of Manipur or anyone else should suffer unless absolutely identified with the assassinations. But, he explained, by long custom all such questions rested with the Viceroy, and it was only because of the gravity of the situation that he had ordered the case of the princes to be brought back to the government at home, to be put before Lord Salisbury the Prime Minister, the Lord Chancellor and the cabinet. In order to restrain the Queen, he continued that he had not wished to ask her for her express approval, or even an expression of opinion from her, as 'in such a painful case as this the whole and express responsibility rests with the Viceroy and your Majesty's ministers'.[13]

Cross informed the Queen that the Viceroy had recommended the commutation of the death sentence in the case of the Regent and of his youngest brother, but not in that of the Senapati and the Thangal General, because in their case the prisoners had been executed after consultation had taken place between them—therefore, under their joint authority. Quite undeterred, the Queen replied:

> the Principle of governing India by fear and <u>crushing</u> them, instead of by firmness and conciliation, <u>is one</u> which will never answer in the end and which the Queen-Empress would wish to see more and more altered. To these reasons the Queen would add that hanging a person (and he a Prince) so long after he has been kept a prisoner has something cruel and cold-blooded about it. These are the Queen-Empress's feelings, which, however she will not write to the Viceroy. She intends neither writing nor saying anything to him about it, as he is evidently very sore about it. The Tongal [Thangal] richly deserves [hanging] though he is eighty-six! He is a very cruel, wicked old man. The other commutations of all the other sentences are quite right.[14]

The Senapati's sentence was due to be carried out on 13 August, and Ghose, his lawyer, now appealed directly to the

---

[13] *Letters and Journals of Queen Victoria*, Esher & Buckle.
[14] *Ibid.*

Queen for clemency for his client. She kept trying to the end, telegraphing Lansdowne on the 12th: 'Baboo, who defended Senapati appeals to me for commutation. Is it possible to do this?'[15] Lansdowne replied that he entertained no doubt that commutation would be a grave public misfortune, and was now absolutely impossible.

The executions of the Senapati and the Thangal General took place the following day, at a quarter to five in the afternoon, near the polo ground and bazaar, and much drama was attached to them. The security was tight, and the execution ground was guarded by 500 rifles of the 2nd and 43rd Gurkhas, who formed a square round the gallows on which the Senapati and Thangal were to be hanged, facing towards each other. Both prisoners were escorted to the gallows by fifty riflemen. The Senapati walked composedly, and climbed the ladder steadily by himself, but the Thangal had to be carried from the jail, and sat on a stool on the platform, instead of standing upright. A description by an English officer of what happened next is published by the Manipur State Archives:

> A sergeant of guard who was executioner tapped the Thangal General on the shoulder and said 'Now then, old man, get up or I can't hang you'. Thangal gazed at him blankly, and then an interpreter translated the remark, on which the old fellow shook his head and roared with laughter. The interpreter said 'Sir, the General states he will not rise' and the Sergeant replied persuasively, 'just tell the old gentleman I'm not going to hurt him'. This, too, was translated, but Thangal would not budge. Then ensued a most ghastly pause whilst a man climbed up to the top of the gallows to lengthen the rope, and when it was adjusted both criminals were loosed off.[16]

In his *History of Manipur*, Roy Jyotirmoy states that in the Rajah's days a criminal sentenced to death was occasionally reprieved if a sufficient number of women appeared to intercede for him. Hoping that this old custom might still prevail, the

---

[15] *Letters and Journals of Queen Victoria*, Esher & Buckle.
[16] Manipur State Archives website, quoting an account by Lieutenant Colonel Alban Wilson.

women of Manipur, particularly the Senapati's relatives, had assembled for the hanging as far as the eye could see, so that the plain was white with women. 'As the drop fell and the Senapati and Thangal General were launched into eternity' there were cries and wailings. 'The stand taken by Tikendrajit and his martyrdom,' writes Jyotirmoy, 'continued to be a source of inspiration to the revolutionaries of Bengal for a long time.'[17]

By the time the Senapati was executed, Ethel had moved down to Hove to stay with Frank's elder brother, Jeffrey, a magistrate, and his wife, Zoe. Also at home was their unmarried daughter, Mabel. The Grimwoods had a comfortable house in First Avenue, Hove with a lady's maid, housemaid, cook and kitchen maid as staff.

Hove would have been very familiar to Ethel, as she and her three younger sisters, Lilian, Beatrice and Sydney,[18] had all been educated there at a small private school run by a widow, a Mrs Moulson, helped by her daughters Emily and Ada, and a French governess.

It was from her brother-in-law's house that Ethel replied to a second letter from the Queen, written by the Hon. Harriet Phipps, her Woman of the Bedchamber:

> Thank you very much for your kind letter. I need not say how very pleased I was to get the photograph of the Queen. Will you kindly convey my very best thanks for it. That I shall value it very greatly & ever remember her kindness to me in my time of trouble seems but a small way of expressing all I feel. The photograph will be doubly valuable to me as it bears Her Majesty's signature.
>
> Will you also thank the Queen for her kind enquiries about my ankle. It is a little better, & the sea bathing seems to strengthen it. I have been greatly distressed at receiving two telegrams from the Senaputty [sic] of Manipur during the last fortnight, begging me to intercede for him. I could of course, do nothing to help him & it is even a relief to me now to know that he is beyond any one's intercession. But I can not forget that he was once my dear Husband's very good friend & my own, & though he deserved his fate, I have still been able to feel sorry for him. I never

---

[17] *History of Manipur*, Roy Jyotirmoy, 1999.
[18] Wrongly described in the 1881 Census as a boy!

considered him responsible for my Husband's terrible death; though he was the murderer of the others, & as such had to suffer. It has been a dreadful time to me, & one that seems to return more vividly to me every day of my life.[19]

The Queen recorded the receipt of the letter in her journal.

Apart from the Senapati and the Thangal General, the government of India decided to exact the extreme penalty in the smallest number of cases, so that only five of the participants were hanged. Although Kulachandra the Regent's and his younger brother Angao Sena's convictions on charges of waging war against the Queen were upheld, they were considered to have been mere tools in the hands of the Senapati and were sentenced to transportation for life. They were sent to the Andaman Islands, and their property confiscated. Zillah Singh was only sent to Sylhet, as were the wives and children of the deposed Maharajah. In all, twenty-two of the rebels were ordered to be transported during the pleasure of the Queen.

It had been much questioned as to how Manipur was to be governed after the rebellion, and whether it would be annexed by the British. It wasn't until the end of September that it was announced, to everyone's surprise and dismay, that a small 5-year-old boy, Churachand Singh, a collateral relative of the ex-Maharajah, had been selected for the throne, rather than the ex-Maharajah's own little son. Major General Johnstone described Churachand as 'an obscure child' and felt that his appointment was a blow to the Royal family, who, until the disaster, had been loyal to the crown. 'Let us beware, we have not heard the last of Manipur!'[20] he wrote dramatically.

Young Churachand's investiture took place on 29 September 1892. He was given the diminished title of 'Rajah' and a smaller salute of 11 guns (gun salutes indicated the importance of a ruler, and varied from 9 to 21: titles went with the number of guns). In fact the choice of Churachand was an astute move on the part of the Government of India, for during his long minority he would

---

[19] RA VIC/N/47/199. By permission of Queen Elizabeth II.
[20] *My Experiences in Manipur*, Major General Sir James Johnstone, 1896.

be looked after by the Political Agent, whose role was seen as 'commanding influence and power'.[21] The Agent would administer the state, and thus be able to bring in reforms. In the case of Manipur this meant the abolition of the old feudal system called 'Lalup', whereby every male over the age of 16, working a rota of ten days out of forty, laboured for the state instead of paying taxes. It was replaced by an annual tax of two rupees on each house.

In appointing Churachand, the government made his position as Rajah hereditary, to descend in direct line provided that in each case it approved the succession. At the same time, it passed a new law 'that every successor to an Indian State holding direct relations with the British Government must be recognised by, or on behalf of, the British Government and no succession is valid unless recognition is given'.[22] Although the choice of Churachand had been so unpopular, the young boy turned out well. He was sent to Mayo, the Princes' College in Ajmer, which had been founded in 1872 for Rajput nobles—an Indian 'Eton'—and was officially crowned when he became 21 in 1908. His popularity increased with the years, and he served his state faithfully until 1916, when he vacated as President in favour of an Indian civil service officer. He kept his title, however, and was restored to being a full Maharajah after the First World War in recognition of the help he had given the allies.

A leading article in *The Times* of 14 August 1891 summed up the Manipur disaster well:

> The general history of the Manipur incident must inspire mingled feelings in the breasts of most Englishmen. The policy in which it originated cannot be said to reflect credit on the Government of India while the actual explosion itself was precipitated by a series of blunders which have never been explained. There seems to be little doubt that had the Government of India made up its mind promptly on the merits of the dynastic struggles between the dethroned Maharajah and his brothers the Senaputtee [*sic*] would hardly have been able to commit the crimes which have

---

[21] *The Indian Political Service*, Terence Creagh Coen, 1971.
[22] *Ibid.*

19 Maharajah Churachand from the Narsing Dynasty during his teenage school days at the Princes' College in Ajmer. (*By kind permission of the Maharaj Kumari Binodini collection*)

cost him his life. But for five months the Government of India seemed to accept the revolution accomplished last September in the palace of Manipur. That revolution was notoriously the work of the Senaputtee although he chose, for his own reasons, to place one of his brothers on the throne. The Government did not indeed assent to the change, but their local representative does not appear to have taken marked steps to express his disapproval. He is said to have tolerated and condoned it to this extent, that he kept up as friendly relations with the new ruler as with the old. On the deplorable mistakes which led up to the massacre, and made it possible, it is unnecessary to dwell. They are still unaccounted for, and so many of the chief actors in that fatal business have perished, that it is more than doubtful whether we shall ever know exactly to whom they were severally due.[23]

---

[23] *The Times*, August 14, 1891, p. 7, col. B.

8

Publication of My Three Years in Manipur

Ethel was still with her brother and sister-in-law when on Tuesday 18 August she received an exciting letter from the publisher George Bentley, whose offices were at New Burlington Street, Piccadilly:

> Dear Madam,
> My son has told me this morning of the interview he had the pleasure of having with you on Saturday. I hope from what he says that the work which you are preparing may make an octavo volume somewhat similar even if smaller to Sir Douglas Forsyth's life, of which work I send you a copy by the same post as this letter goes by, and of which I beg your acceptance.[1] It is rather important that the book should come before the public at as early date as possible, that it may not be preceded by the accounts of others, if any such be contemplated. I am prepared to take the risk of the publication, & to divide equally with you the profits which may arise from the publication.[2]

Ethel must have started to write *My Three Years in Manipur and Escape from the Recent Mutiny* almost as soon as she reached safety. It is the only work to have been published about the disaster, apart from the official records, and therefore her first-hand account is a unique and vital contribution to its history. She had to write it, as she explains, without the benefit of a single scrap of paper to remind her of the facts, as she had lost everything in the retreat. The book is also an interesting insight into Ethel's own

---

[1] This must have been Forsyth's *Autobiography*.
[2] B/L: Bentley Papers Add. 46645, p.703.

character—on the one hand she was a Victorian woman expecting the protection of her husband, on the other someone tough enough to endure great physical hardship.

My Three Years in Manipur is written with much charm and humour, and vividly evokes the life of a Victorian woman posted to a remote part of the empire who is unexpectedly thrown into the turmoil of battle. It divides into two parts, of which the first is devoted to a lively account of the Grimwoods' first few months in Manipur before the disaster. Ethel explains that their reactions to Frank's appointment as Political Officer were quite different. To her it meant being mistress of a Residency with servants dressed in scarlet and gold and 'V.R.' incised on their buttons, while Frank's thoughts were full of sport: wild duck shoots, polo matches and tiger-hunting.

Ethel recounts how when they first went to Manipur (which is how she always refers to it, rather than Imphal), the 44th Gurkha Rifles were stationed just four miles away at the fort at Langthabal, so the officers provided them with plenty of company for tennis matches, teas and her 'at homes'. On these occasions the Maharajah would lend his band to play for them, and Ethel marvelled at the ease with which the musicians, composed entirely of Nagas, picked up English music of all kinds. She emphasised the hospitality given to all visitors:

> You only have to be English to be assured of a welcome from your countrymen, who are ready to put themselves, their houses, and possessions all at your service. There are disadvantages, maybe, to be met with in India which are many and great, and one loses much by having to live out there; but one never meets with such true-hearted kindness anywhere else as in India. The narrow prejudices and questioning doubts as to who you are, and what your station in life is, which assail you at home, vanish entirely when you need hospitality.[3]

The Grimwoods were unhappy when the 44th Gurkhas were moved away on a Chin expedition and not replaced, throwing them entirely on the princes for company, although they

---

[3] *My Three Years in Manipur*, Ethel Grimwood, 1891.

PUBLICATION OF *MY THREE YEARS IN MANIPUR*

20 The Vandyk photograph of Ethel used as a frontispiece to *My Three Years in Manipur*, the book she published about her experiences in November, 1891. *(author)*

socialised happily with them. Ethel describes how at the Maharajah's request Frank gave him English lessons in the afternoons, and how he used to read out of an old spelling book, filled with a very odd selection of phrases such as 'an elegant puce quilt'. He found the latter word unpronounceable, and it always ended up as 'kilt'. He mastered 'goodbye', but used it interchangeably with 'hello'![4]

Ethel and Frank delighted in the little menagerie of animals and birds they had gathered, among them grey and red cranes, otters, monkeys, deer and a bear. There is a delightful woodcut of a bear on the title page of *My Three Years in Manipur*, and Ethel describes how they had adopted it when it was a small ball of cuddlesome black fluff. However:

> He got very fierce as he grew older, and one day I was out in the garden gathering flowers and suddenly noticed the Chuppressies and orderlies flying towards the house—a proceeding that always happened directly the bear was at large. He very soon spied me out, and came rushing towards me, and I began to run; but long before I had got to the house he had overtaken me. I threw the flowers I had collected behind me, hoping that he would stop for them, but he just sniffed at them and then came on. He caught me up in a moment and clawed at my back, and tore my jacket all the way down. Fortunately it was a very cold day, and I had put on a thick winter coat, which saved me from getting badly clawed; but he gave me some nasty scratches. Luckily the Ghoorka orderly saw it from the house, and ran up and beat him off; and then the other servants came and captured him and chained him up.[5]

The next day the bear was taken away and released from captivity on a nearby hill. When Ethel's book came out, the story appealed to the editor of the *Child's Companion* (published by the Religious Tract Society), who begged to include it in his magazine. He was given permission by Bentley, who charged him four shillings for using the electro-plate of the woodcut.

Ethel and Frank particularly loved their garden, which was tended by nine Naga gardeners, or 'malis'. Ethel tells with

---

[4] *My Three Years*, Grimwood.
[5] Ibid.

amusement how a spinster friend was so shocked at learning that they gardened with little on but their necklaces, that she sent nine pairs of striped bathing-drawers for them to wear. A few days later Ethel went into the garden to find one enterprising mali had converted his into a jacket and another was sporting his as a turban, so she gave up trying! Her own dress created much curiosity in the distant villages they visited, some of whose inhabitants had not seen an Englishwoman before. The women would come up and touch her clothes, and even imagined that the fullness at the back of her dress concealed a tail!

As well as the Residency, the Grimwoods had a hill bungalow where they went most weekends—Saturday until Tuesday. It was fifteen miles from Manipur and about 6,000 feet above sea-level, so delightfully cool all year round. They also owned several villages given them by the Maharajah, the inhabitants of which worked for them, and were paid for their labour. Ethel tells how she and Frank would ride to their bungalow on horseback. On one occasion the Nagas, wishing to honour them, put up a triumphal arch at the entrance to their garden. By chance she happened to glance up before riding under, and saw to her horror the newly cut off head of a dog hanging as its centrepiece, with his paws and tail gracing the sides. Dogs were highly regarded by the Nagas, who considered them a delicacy to eat.

The weather from the end of April (when the monsoon broke) to the end of October was the rainy season in Manipur, while the months from November to March were perfect—cool, but with bright sunshine. During the good weather Ethel and Frank would go off to camp for a month at a time, only returning to the Residency for a few days in between. Putting Ethel's descriptions together, they seem to have been away from the Residency a good deal more than they were there.

Ethel must have worked quickly to have *My Three Years in Manipur* ready for publication by November. It may be that she found writing it a therapeutic way of recovering from the trauma of her terrifying experiences in the Residency and the flight. As generally happens with people who have suffered a severe shock, her accounts differ slightly between what she wrote to her sister-in-law Mabel immediately on reaching safety, and what she describes in her book. Despite these discrepancies Ethel certainly did not deserve the attacks made on her veracity by Lieutenant Colonel St. John Michell, who had questioned her on her arrival in Cachar and formed the opinion that her account of what happened was a tissue of lies. Claiming that 'no one was in a position to speak with more authority than himself',[6] Michell voiced his views of Ethel at the end of an astonishing letter written from Ceylon to Sir H. M. Durand, the military member of the Governor-General's Council on 14 August 1891, now in the National Archives:

> Mrs. Grimwood acted most injudiciously before the disaster especially in writing to the Jubraj[7] (she carefully abstains from mentioning this fact). Her account of the hospital running with blood, etc. is absolutely incorrect. She was never wounded or under fire for the lower rooms of the Residency are shot proof, only two or three shots were fired at the retreating party at long distance. She seriously embarrassed our officers by entreating them to retire. She never showed anyone the way, for there was no way to show, the road being perfectly straight and well-known to all. Her relations with her husband were very strained, and it is quite possible he never spoke to her. In no way did she act heroically. ... I fancy Mrs. Grimwood's story must be pretty well exploded at home by this time for when I heard the hat was coming round for her I wrote to two old friends of mine on the staff of the Duke of Cambridge [Commander-in-Chief of the British Army] and the Duke of Connaught, and told them the truth. The poor lady is not much to blame. It is a case of heredity. You came out to India after me, some time I think, but when I came out Mrs. Charley Moore was a very well-known lady...[8]

It is possible that Michell may have been distantly related to Ethel's family through Boisragon, Ethel's mother's first husband. Michell, who was elderly and nearing retirement, seems to have had a personal grudge against the Moore family, as well as Ethel. His letter shows no regard for the fact that she had lived through a terrifying experience, endured a gruelling march, and learned at

---

[6] N/A PRO 30/40/12/3.
[7] The Jubraj was the Senapati's official title.
[8] N/A PRO 30/40/12/3.

the end of it that her husband had been murdered. Part of his antipathy towards Ethel may be that he believed she had warned the Senapati of the danger he was in, with all the tragic consequences. Whether she did, we shall never know. In her book she writes 'before the Durbar the officers were joking with me, and trying to find out whether I were in the secret or not'. She then describes the intricacies of translating the written orders of the Government of India into Manipuri:

> for this purpose two of the office clerks and the Burmese interpreter were brought to the Residency and given the papers to translate. The orders were lengthy, and the translation of them took some time. Each of the clerks had a sentry placed over him, and they all had to swear an oath that they would not divulge one word to anyone of the contents of the papers given them to translate. Some time before they were completed the Regent and *all* his brothers arrived at the gate. I have laid particular stress on the word *all*, because it has been said that the Jubraj (Senapati) did not accompany his brother on this occasion, though subsequent evidence has since appeared showing that he was really present with the rest.[9]

Against Michell's judgement must be set the fact that all those who escaped with Ethel unanimously praised her for her help and courage; nor would she have been given the Royal Red Cross without her story being verified. Her account was, inevitably, embroidered by the press, who seized on the disaster, which they renamed 'The Manipur Outrage', and blew up some of the incidents to excess, while inventing others. For example *The Englishman*, published in Calcutta on 4 May, circulated two stories. The first was that Captain Butcher and Ethel were dragging their way up a hill, the last in the line, when the enemy suddenly appeared in pursuit, and Butcher, taking a rifle from a sepoy, fired over her body, as she lay down before him, with 'unerring aim' hitting five men without a miss. The second story was that Butcher, before the stockade was rushed, had turned to Ethel and said that he had 'reserved two cartridges, and that if the advancing men proved to

---

[9] *My Three Years*, Grimwood.

be Manipuris he intended one of the cartridges for her and the other for himself'.[10] Both stories appear to be questionable.

Ethel seems to have been well aware of the criticisms against her, and wrote:

> It has been said lately by some that this retreat to Cachar was in a great measure due to my presence in Manipur at the time, and that my helplessness has been the means of dragging the good name of the army, and the Gurkha corps in particular, through the mire, by strongly influencing the officers in their decision to effect 'the stampede to Cachar'. But I scarcely think that they would have allowed the presence of, and danger to one woman to deter them from whatever they considered their duty; and had they decided to remain at the Residency that night, I should never have questioned their right to do so, even as I raised no argument for or against the retreat to Cachar. I think that the honour of England is as dear to us women as it is to the men; and though it is not our vocation in life to be soldiers, and to fight for our country, yet when occasion offers, I have little doubt that the women of England have that in them which would enable them to come out of any dilemma as nobly and honourably as the men and with just as much disregard for their own lives as the bravest soldier concerned. But such an insinuation as I have quoted is not, I am happy to think, the unspoken opinion of the many to whom the story of Manipur is familiar. It is but the uncharitable verdict of a few.[11]

Ethel's vivid account of the disaster makes her book a dramatic record of events, although throughout it she claims very little for herself. She mentions that she knew the road, but only because she had often made the journey along it and was 'able to give the others the benefit of my knowledge'.[12] She had also been able to recognise the Leimatak peak, and pointed it out to the others. Her understanding of spoken Manipuri had proved very useful, too, when they had come across the native sepoys cooking their meal, and she had been enabled to glean from them that Captain Cowley's troop was still ahead of them.

Ethel's book gives no hint of any strain in her marriage: she and

---

[10] *The Englishman*, 4 May 1891.
[11] *My Three Years*, Grimwood.
[12] *Ibid*.

PUBLICATION OF *MY THREE YEARS IN MANIPUR*

Frank seem to have been on good terms, and to have talked to each other freely. He was, perhaps, with his love of sport, more of a 'man's man' than she would have wished, but of his death she wrote touchingly, 'I cannot dwell on this part of the story. It is all too recent and painful as yet, and too vivid in my recollection.'[13]

Bentley worked very hard to get *My Three Years in Manipur* ready for publication in November, sending a telegram about the technicalities to the printer, Keith Johnston at Dilling & Sons, Guildford, as late as 6 November 1891: 'The Manipur cancels will be thirty-seven,' he wrote. 'One sixty five as arranged. One twenty nine and one seventy five since added. You need not make thirty three or thirty five. Will post two cancels referred to.'[14] On 16 November it was recorded in Bentley's ledgers that the large sum of £365 had been spent on advertising *My Three Years in Manipur*, which sold for 15 shillings a copy. It was printed in octavo, and beautifully bound with a watermark-style cover and gold-stamped leather spine and corners. The illustrations were largely the same excellent ones as had appeared in the *Illustrated London News*. German publishers showed a great interest in the book, and Tauchnitz of Leipzig, with Bentley's agreement, brought out an edition printed in English in 1891. This was rather smaller in size and was without any illustrations apart from having Ethel's photograph as the frontispiece.[15]

The Times, reviewing *My Three Years in Manipur* on 16 November 1891, described it as a 'simple but thrilling narrative of deplorable disaster and heroic endurance'. Ethel was praised for the 'clear, straightforward account she had given, without advancing opinions of her own'. The reviewer continued, 'This is a story that can only be told in her own words, and could not be told more modestly or impressively.' Ethel had kept herself 'so spontaneously in the background that it is almost an effort to realise that this is a woman's story of her own brave deeds and still braver endurances. Only at the close of her story of the retreat

---

[13] *My Three Years*, Grimwood.
[14] B/L Bentley Papers Add. 46645 p. 731.
[15] B/L, Tauch 2796.

do the feelings of a woman break forth in a narrative which is otherwise studiously impersonal and self-forgetful'.[16]

The reviewer defended Frank Grimwood, commenting that the book

> reflects but little credit on those who were responsible for the policy pursued. At any rate there is nothing in Mrs. Grimwood's account to disallow the conclusion that her husband and the other victims of the disaster were sacrificed to a series of blunders. It is more clear than ever that the policy of arresting and deporting the Senapati while recognizing the [then] Jubraj as Maharajah, which Mr. Quinton was sent to Manipur to carry out, was from the outset thoroughly disapproved and even cordially detested by Mr. Grimwood. It is no clearer than before why he was kept in ignorance of it until the last moment, when it was too late to protest effectively, and why his judgement was so peremptorily overruled. What seems certain, however, is that Mr. Quinton was as little responsible for the policy which ended in disaster as Mr. Grimwood himself. He was merely acting in execution of orders given him by the Government of India.[17]

The *Illustrated London News* agreed with *The Times* that the great charm of Ethel's book was its simplicity and freshness of observation. They praised her for the absence of any repining, and admired the fact that she showed no resentment against the princes, and did not use the word 'murder' in reference to the tragedy. To the reviewer, the whole point of the book seemed to rest on the fact that the Grimwoods and the princely family had lived on terms of friendship, and would have continued to do so if the government of India had not interfered: 'Public opinion in this country with regard to that transaction was never very favourable to the Indian government,' the reviewer commented. Ethel had told her story with 'graphic energy ... the whole of her simple and modest narrative ... will preserve her name in the esteem and admiration of her countrymen and countrywomen'.[18]

My Three Years in Manipur was an instant success, quickly

---

[16] *The Times*, 16 November 1891, p.10.
[17] *Ibid*.
[18] *Illustrated London News*, November 28 1891, p.708.

becoming a bestseller. It ran into three editions, and made Ethel a substantial amount of money. In 1891 alone she earned £744.19.10 as her half share of the profits, with a further sum of £71.1.10 the following year, and with small amounts still being paid into her account up to 1898. This compared very well with another of Bentley's best-selling authors, the prolific Marie Corelli, who received £855 6s. from the five books she published between 1892 and 1893.

Ethel was well aware of the aftermath of tragedy left for so many by the Manipur rebellion, ending her book:

> But in more than one home in England there is sorrow for those who are not. Their vacant places can never be filled up, even though in time, when the grass has grown green above them, we shall learn to think of them not as dead, but as living elsewhere purer, truer, freer lives, unhampered by the sorrows and cares of the world. Time may, perhaps, do that for us, but meanwhile hearts will ache, and longings will arise for the 'touch of a vanished hand, and the sound of a voice that is still', and the hard lesson will have to be learned that nothing is our own—no, not even those who seem part of our very lives, around whom all our tenderest interests and highest hopes cling. Well for us if, in learning the lesson, we keep our faith and trust in the Being for whose pleasure we were created, and whose right it is to demand from us what we value most. And if, when our time comes, and we look back across the vista of years at all the disappointments and all the sorrows, which, after all, outweigh the happiness in our lives, and can say, 'It was all for the best,' then the lesson will not have been learnt in vain, and it will indeed be well with us.[19]

---

[19] *My Three Years*, Grimwood.

9

A New World

In the spring of 1892 a very large portrait of Ethel was exhibited at the Royal Academy. It was the work of John Hanson Walker, a successful Victorian portraitist who, when still a boy, had been befriended by the great Frederic Leighton, later President of the Royal Academy, and had become his model and protégé. Walker had already painted another interesting subject with Indian connections: the Hon. Sir Ashley Eden, Lieutenant Governor of Bengal, 1877–82, whose portrait was shown at the Royal Academy exhibition of 1883.[1] It seems that Walker, reading Ethel's story, may have seized the opportunity to ask her to sit for him, for *The Times*, in reviewing the exhibition, wrote: 'Mr. Hanson Walker is to be congratulated on his good fortune in securing Mrs. Frank Grimwood as a sitter. He has repaid the debt by painting a much better portrait than he has ever painted before.'[2]

Walker, who was my great-grandfather, painted Ethel three-quarter length, standing with her hands clasped in front of her, looking over her right shoulder. The portrait, which is now in my possession, successfully captures her somewhat 'gamin' looks, upturned nose, clear grey eyes and bobbed curly hair, which give the impression that when young she could have been something of a tomboy.

Although Walker shows Ethel clearly wearing her Royal Red Cross medal on her left shoulder, the entry in the Royal Academy catalogue mistakenly read: 'Mrs. Frank Grimwood dressed in

---

[1] This now hangs in the Bengal Chamber of Commerce & Industry, Calcutta.
[2] Review of Royal Academy, *The Times*, Saturday 22 May 1892, p.6.

21 Ethel's portrait by John Hanson Walker, exhibited at the Royal Academy in 1892: the catalogue wrongly described her as wearing the V.C. rather than the Royal Red Cross. *(author)*

black and wearing the *V.C.*' It is odd, in the light of all the publicity Ethel had received, that Walker or the Academy should have made this mistake. Confusion may have arisen due to articles such as that published in the *Illustrated London News* of 7 June 1891, which, having described how Ethel had won her medal, continued, 'If the Government could have seen their way to bestow the *Victoria Cross* on Mrs. Grimwood the general approbation would have been complete.' A further letter in the *Pioneer* also suggested that she should have won the V.C. rather than the Royal Red Cross.

Over the years the portrait disappeared from view, and my search for it proved both exhaustive and exciting. It started with a complete blank, as no trace of it could be found in England. Only one person abroad knew of the hunt, who by a fortunate chance was Robert Stewart, the then Senior Curator of Painting and Sculpture at the National Portrait Gallery, Washington, D.C. In February 1987, I received a letter from him enclosing a photograph of a portrait of (as he described it) 'a lady wearing the Russian order of St. Vladimir'. He had seen the picture hanging in the gallery of a Washington art dealer friend, and had noticed that it was signed 'Walker' in the lower left corner. Although the first name was indistinct, he was curious. 'If this isn't your Walker,' wrote Stewart, 'I thought you might have an idea which Walker painted it?'[3] Although the portrait was undated, the dress and hair-do suggested the late 1880s. The dealer had bought it at Sloan's sale rooms, Washington, D.C. because he collected White Russian memorabilia, and had thought that the medal the woman was wearing was the order of St. Vladimir, and that she might have been the wife of a British Ambassador to St. Petersburg. The portrait had been sent to auction by a Mrs Moeser of Virginia, who had inherited it from her brother's estate. Her brother had travelled extensively and had been a keen collector of art, but she did not know anything more about it.

The response to Robert Stewart had to be quick, as my

---

[3] Letter of 17 February 1987 from the late Robert Stewart, Curator of Painting, National Portrait Gallery, Washington, D.C.

biography of John Hanson Walker was just going to print![4] An image of the Royal Red Cross was faxed to him, and he confirmed that it was indeed the medal the woman was wearing. Comparing the portrait with a photograph of Ethel, he was without doubt that it was her.

In commenting on Walker's portrait, Robert Stewart said that he liked the way the artist had depicted Ethel. Her pose was natural, but had he, when painting her, been thinking of Reynolds' S-curve of beauty? Had he consciously intended to portray Ethel, who wears black, as a virtuous widow—a kind of Penelopean ideal? Her jewellery also interested him, for besides an expensive-looking bracelet on her left arm, Ethel has two brooches pinned opposite her medal—a half-moon cross, and a star above it; he thought the latter might be of Indian origin, as it showed a Muslim influence. One thing he was certain of was that the stones were real, for as he explained, at that time a woman in Ethel's position would have scorned paste. She seems to have had a fondness for jewellery, for in the beautiful photograph of her taken by Herbert Barraud in 1891 she wears a different bracelet, and several rings on her wedding ring finger. Clothes obviously interested her too, for (according to *The Lady* of 1891) her dress is in the height of fashion, with a low neck, large leg of mutton sleeves drawn in at the elbow, and a 'wasp' waist.

Judging by the two likenesses of Ethel in the *Illustrated London News*, Walker has flattered her a little. Photographs such as the one by Vandyk which forms the frontispiece to *My Three Years in Manipur* show her lips to be thicker, and her look prosaic rather than dreamy. Walker's portrait is very large (185 cms × 96.5 cms) and this prompted Stewart to think that it might have originally been commissioned for a pre-arranged space.

A visitor to Winchester College, or to Merton College, Oxford, will find memorials to Frank in both places. As early as May 1891 *The Wykehamist* suggested he should be honoured by a plaque in the school's cloister, and in due course a brass plaque was erected

---

[4] *John Hanson Walker, The Life and Times of a Victorian Artist*, Belinda Morse, 1987.

to him in that part of the cloister devoted to those who died young. It reads:

> In memory of
> FRANK ST. CLAIR GRIMWOOD ICS
> 2nd son of Jeffrey Grimwood Grimwood
> late Commoner of this College and of
> Merton College Oxford
> Deputy Commissioner of Assam and
> British Resident at Manipur
> where he was treacherously murdered
> 24th March 1891 aged 37.

At Merton College, Frank is commemorated in the ante-chapel, with a different inscription:

> Frank St. Clair Grimwood
> Sometime Postmaster of Merton College
> Born 18 January 1854
> died a soldier's death
> at the Manipur Residency
> 24 March 1891
> Whilst doing high political duty
> Righteously and fearlessly
> on the frontier of the Indian Empire
> Remembered with love and admiration
> by his Oxford friends.

One wonders how much hand Ethel or Frank's family had in composing the words. Ethel seems to have had far warmer and closer relations with the Grimwoods than her own parents, who get no mention at all in her book. By the time of the disaster her mother seems to have vanished, and her father had remarried a much younger woman.

Years before, Ethel's parents had caused a sensation in Indian society by their marriage, for in 1864 Charles Moore had run off with her mother, Margaret Emma (born Gerrard, in Ireland) and had been cited as co-respondent by Theodore Boisragon, Margaret Emma's first husband. The case was made even more notorious because Boisragon (who was later to become a Major General) had been one of the first to take advantage of the new 'Matrimonial Causes Act' of 1857 in suing for divorce.

Having had only one son, Alan, by Boisragon, Margaret Emma presented Moore with four daughters, of whom Ethel was the eldest. After the birth of her fourth daughter, Sydney, in India in 1873 she disappears from all records. She may have died in childbirth, departed the fold, or been a victim, like so many who lived in India at that time, of cholera, malaria or the climate. She had not been present when Ethel married Frank in 1887, for only her father, then a judge in the Indian Civil Service, signed the register, together with her second sister, Lilian.

It can be seen from this and the census of 1891 that at the time of the disaster Ethel had no family of her own to whom she was close enough to turn for support. Her father, Charles, aged 53, had retired and was 'living on his own means' with his new wife, Elizabeth, who was a mere seven years older than Ethel herself. The Moores shared two London houses, numbers 38 and 39 Margaret Street, Cavendish Square, with several other occupants: John Moore, a 62-year-old coachmaker, his wife Louise, their daughters, Laura and Frances (both corset makers), and Emily and Evelyn Leake, spinster sisters. From this it does not appear that Charles was particularly well off. His finances would have been further strained by the fact that he was keeping a mistress, a Miss Emily Barnett, at 118 Beaufort Street, Chelsea. In reality, 'Miss' Barnett was the wife of 54-year-old Charles Mudstone, described as 'born in Calcutta and living on his own means'. When Charles Moore died in December 1898 he claimed in his will that Emily's son, baptised Charles William after him, was his own. The boy would only have been twelve at the time of the disaster.

When Charles Moore made his will three weeks before his death he was still living at Margaret Street, but gave the Oriental Club, Hanover Square, as a second address. His two executors were William Lambe, a fellow member of the club, and his brother, Major Martin James Moore. The will was complicated by the fact that at some time previously, Charles had mortgaged shares given to him by his two surviving brothers, Colonel John Arthur Henry Moore Brabazon and Martin Moore, to Lambe, which on his death had to be redeemed. His wife and youngest daughter, Sydney, were to receive one quarter each of the income thus raised, but Ethel and her two sisters were cut out of their father's will entirely, as he claimed that they were already married and well provided for.[5] Instead he left the rest of the estate to Charles William, his illegitimate son, on attaining the age of twenty-one.

Somewhat surprisingly, two and a half years after Charles Moore's death his brother Martin and his wife Susannah moved into Beaufort Street with Emily, who now described herself as 'Emily *Moore*, widow'. Her son, who was 22, had also changed his surname to Moore, and was working as a bank clerk. Had Charles therefore made a death-bed marriage to Emily?

The tangled skein of her father's life may not have affected Ethel over much, for, after six years of widowhood, she took the plunge and married again. Her second husband was Andrew Cornwall Miller of Carshalton, Surrey. He was 26, and therefore one year younger than her. Only her third sister, Beatrice (now Mrs Ainslie), and her youngest sister, Sydney, were present at the wedding ceremony on 30 May 1895 held at the Registry Office, St.George's Hanover Square. A Grimwood descendant remembered that Frank's family were not happy at Ethel's choice of husband, feeling that she had married beneath her socially, even though Andrew's father had been an army colonel. How Ethel met Andrew is unknown, although it may have been through her half-brother, Alan Boisragon, who had married a Surrey girl from nearby Reigate two years earlier.

At the time of their wedding Andrew Miller was the proprietor of Mill House Paper Mill, Carshalton, which he had taken over the previous year, having possibly, before that, been in the army. The mill, an old one founded in 1817, was on the river Wandle, and employed six men making 'First Class handmade papers' with a weekly output of six tons. Miller's tenure, however, was

---

[5] Moore's will was proved on 22 March 1899 and the exact amount left registered as £9,674 11s.

The women's market, Imphal remains unchanged since Ethel's day. Photo courtesy Author

The Manipur Polo Club players. Photo courtesy Author

Above: The walls enclosing the old palace. Photo courtesy Author

Left: The border town of Mao Thana today.

Photo courtesy Author

The 'Pung Cholom'. Photo courtesy Author

The classical dancers of the Manipur Dance Academy. Photo courtesy Author

The memorial to those who were murdered in the 'Manipur Disaster'. It stands in the grounds of the old residency, now the governor's palace. Photo courtesy Ayai Shimray

The Maharajah's Palace Imphal built for the boy Rajah Churachand by the British 1904. Photo courtesy William Clark

short-lived, for by 1900 he had given it up, and in 1906 it was closed altogether.

Four years after their marriage, Andrew emigrated to America, leaving Ethel to follow him two years later. By 1910 they were living in the Cascades district of Clackamas, Oregon on the southern outskirts of Portland. If the census return is accurate, Andrew had become a naturalised American citizen,[6] but appears to have had no set job, although he was in the right area to be involved in some way in the paper industry. Ethel had not taken up American citizenship, preferring instead to remain an 'alien'. She must have found their new home with its proximity to the 11,239-feet snow-covered Mount Hood in eastern Clackamas county a nostalgic reminder of the hills and mountains of Manipur. However, the pleasure was not to last, for sadly her marriage to Andrew proved unhappy, and they separated.

Ethel then vanishes from all records until ten years later, when in 1920, she was to be found living at Second Street, Newport, Oregon,[7] a city on the scenic Pacific coast, where there are rough seas and rocky tidal pools with anemones, starfish, crabs and molluscs. Although these delights were so near at hand she may not have had time to enjoy them, as she was now badly off, despite the generous pension and other allowances accorded her as a young widow. She was on her own, teaching music for a living, and making a little extra on the side by having a boarder, Richard Chatterton. He was a marine engineer, aged 31, and single. His father was American, but his mother, like Ethel's, had been born in Ireland. What his relationship was to the now 53-year-old Ethel is enigmatic.

In recreating her life in the United States Ethel invented a new persona for herself, calling herself 'Evelyn' Miller. She had become well-known as a talented musician, teaching music to 'most of the young inhabitants of Newport'[8] who, perhaps, made up for the children with which she had never been blessed.

---

[6] 1910 US census return, Cascades District, Clackamas County, Oregon. Naturalisation required a minimum five-year residency in the country.
[7] US census 1920, Newport, Lincoln County, Oregon.
[8] *Yaquina Bay Times*, Newport, Oregon, 16 August 1928.

As the years went by, 'Evelyn' began to suffer ill health and mental troubles. After the disaster she had confided to her sister-in-law Mabel, 'I think the horrors of those hours will last to the end of my life'[9] and this seems to have been all too true. Who knows what terrors she endured, or what unhappiness from her broken marriage? What nightmares whirled through her head in the dark hours? She began to suffer delusions, hallucinations and mental confusion which she was incapable of understanding or controlling.

As her mind began to give way, Ethel moved for treatment from Newport to Albany, where she became an inmate in 'Dr. House's sanitorium for mental care'. She then moved once more to Portland, perhaps for further treatment, and died there on 11 August 1928, aged 55, of 'toxic psychosis'.[10]

'Evelyn' was still able to write in a clear hand when she made her will on 27 August 1926. Although she signed it 'Evelyn Miller', she preceded this with 'Ethel', writing it in as if as an afterthought. She named her second sister, Lilian (now Mrs W. B. Maxwell), of Albert Court, Kensington Gardens, as her next of kin, and the local newspaper quoted Lilian as saying that she 'had hoped to take her back to England'.[11]

Ethel's life was one of drama to the end. In her will she left all she had to a young man of 31 called Floyd Wilson, whom she named as her sole beneficiary as well as executor. Perhaps Floyd had given her friendship in her loneliness, or acted as a chauffeur and handyman to her, for he later ran a tyre re-capping and repair service.

After Ethel's death Floyd moved to Ashland, Oregon, where he was a keen member of the Church of Christ-Christian until his death in 1982 at the age of 85. Sadly he received nothing from Evelyn's will, as her estate was declared insolvent after expenses

---

[9] Letter written from Lahkipur, Cachar 2 April 1891. RA VIC/N/47/175. By permission of Queen Elizabeth II.
[10] Death certificate issued Portland, Oregon, State Reg. 2231. Toxic psychosis is 'a serious mental disorder characterized by illusions, delusions, hallucinations, mental confusion and a lack of insight on the part of the patient into his or her condition' (*Chambers Dictionary*).
[11] *Yaquina Bay Times*, Newport, Oregon, 16 August 1928, p.4.

had been paid. The inventory of her possessions showed that besides her two pianos (an upright and baby grand), she owned practically nothing, apart from a few ornaments, some clothes, books and linen. Her jewellery (valued at $119.30) now only consisted of a ruby ring, a silver pendant and two brooches. A second diamond and ruby ring had been pawned for $150 to pay for medical expenses. The entire estate was valued at no more than $300.

At this last sad stage of her life, Andrew Miller suddenly reappeared, paying, through his lawyers in London, all the expenses of his wife's last illness and funeral, for although he and Ethel had separated, they had never actually divorced. Possibly Andrew had been responsible for the loss of her money during their brief marriage, and now felt obliged to make amends.

Ethel must have once been popular in Newport, for when advance notice of the funeral was published in the local newspaper on 15 August, 'all her friends' were invited to attend. The paper also carried a notice asking 'Victoria and Vancouver papers to copy'.[12] This may be because her third sister, Beatrice Ainslie, had emigrated to British Columbia, and had sons who would now be in their thirties.

A small piece in the *Yaquina Bay Times*, Newport, mentioned Ethel's past heroism as a lingering but inaccurate memory: 'Years ago Mrs. Miller rendered distinctive service to her country by leading an army unit through a short cut so that they could fortify themselves and battle with the opposing enemy. They were victorious due to her knowledge of the country, and the British government repaid her by granting her an annuity for life'[13]

It is interesting that the memory that Ethel's knowledge of the terrain between Manipur and Cachar had helped in the escape from the Residency was the strongest to survive. It may be that as the years went by her account of her ordeal got a little exaggerated, but nothing could take away from the fact of her heroism, and her innate modesty about it. As she herself wrote in *My*

---

[12] *Oregonian*, Portland, Oregon, 15 August 1928, p.9.
[13] *Yaquina Bay Times*, 16 August 1928, p. 4.

Three Years in Manipur: 'That such praise has been bestowed is more than sufficient reward for what, after all, many another Englishwoman would have done under similar circumstances.'

10

In Ethel's Footsteps

Nowadays it is easier for a camel to go through the eye of a needle than for a foreigner to enter Manipur, for it is a 'restricted area', and individuals are not normally granted permits. It was thanks to the British Legion and the protection of the Indian army's Assam Rifles that my husband and I were able to go there in April 2006. We were with a party of eight veterans, all of whom had fought with General Slim's 14th army, men now in their eighties, but straight-backed, quick-witted, and excellent talkers. They had been enabled to return to the scene of their battles under the auspices of the British Legion thanks to the 'Heroes Return' scheme, funded by the government through the lottery for two years. Also with us were those who had lost fathers in the campaign when they were too young to remember them, and were visiting their graves for the first time. The fallen are buried in the war cemeteries of Kohima and Imphal, and are commemorated at the former with the famous lines, 'When you go home tell them of us and say, for your tomorrow we gave our today.'

Both Kohima and Imphal returned to the headlines during the Second World War, when the allied forces under General Slim turned the tide of war there against the invading Japanese in 1944. Slim's book *Defeat into Victory* recounts in graphic detail the battles on the Kohima ridge and the successful hard-fought defence of the Imphal plain, where at one point the encircling Japanese hooked round to the west, so that some of the fiercest fighting took place round Bishenpur on the track from Imphal to Silchar, and among the hills over which Ethel had made her escape fifty years earlier.

It was intensely moving to travel with Stan, Dan, Len, Harry, John, Bill, Ian and Ken, veterans of the campaign, and, as we went, to hear them suddenly recall memories of battles fought at a particular point on the road. Speaking gently, even humorously, they would tell of small events that seemed large at the time, such as their delight at the capture of a double-seated Japanese field lavatory—a great improvement on the empty explosive boxes in general use—which they thereafter proudly towed after them.

We quickly realised that our entry to Manipur would not be secure until the last moment. Travelling with us were Roy and Barbara, who were making their second attempt to visit the country. The year before they had received their hard-won permits, only to be turned away at Imphal airport because they had been sent photocopies of them rather than the originals.

For us, too, it was touch and go, as the day before our party was due to travel down from Kohima to Imphal our organisers were warned that the road would be blockaded the next day, and was therefore forbidden to us! Fortunately (they never told us how), the British Legion persuaded the authorities to change their minds, but we found that our vehicle was the only one on the road that day apart from our military escort!

The solitude of the road enabled us to enjoy with even greater pleasure the breathtaking scenery of the first part of our journey, where we passed through mountain range after mountain range, stretching into the distance as far as the eye could see. To our left was a vertiginous drop, at the bottom of which we could just make out stretches of watery paddy field far below.

The road, descending steeply all the way to Imphal, had crumbled away altogether in places, so that after an hour or two we began to regard our driver as a hero, amazed at his skill in negotiating all the hazards as he braved floods and jumped the coach around potholed hairpin bends only to find the road ahead had collapsed altogether. Several graves by the roadside reminded us of other travellers who had been less lucky.

At last we bumped our way into Mao Thana, the frontier town between Nagaland and Manipur, Mao being the name of one of Manipur's tribes. Here we began a nervous wait while our documents were searched, checked and re-checked. In the Grimwoods' day, Mao Thana had been just a collection of huts with a rest house, but it is now a bustling mountain town, its main street lined with small hotels, so small that one wonders how some of them can provide enough space to lie down! In front of the hotels are stalls with colourful fruit, vegetables and flowers beautifully arranged in baskets: luscious apples, onions, potatoes, tomatoes, garlic, ginger, and long green curry beans—a very appealing sight. Colourful, too, are the parked lorries, whose chassis are painted in bright geometrical designs: what a cheerful impression they would make on our own motorways!

As we walked along the street, which was largely populated with soldiers, I was reminded that it was through Mao Thana that Ethel and Frank had ridden with sadness on their way to Jorehat, in Assam, where they had been sent on being replaced at Imphal by the unfortunate Mr Heath. As it was a border town then too, it was there that their escort, the Thangal General's son, had left them. Their journey on horseback to Kohima had taken them eight days; even with modern transport it took us almost twelve hours.

Describing their journey, Ethel had written: 'the scenery between Kohima and Manipur is magnificent'. We found this to be quite true, and felt that the countryside and villages we passed must hardly have changed since her time. We caught several glimpses of them: groups of scattered houses built of wood, mud plaster and bamboo, each with their own verandah, and standing in a small compound. Although some have retained their traditional thatched roofs, these have often now been replaced by corrugated iron, in some cases held down by stones to resist the high winds.

After Mao Thana the mountains subside gently into hills clothed with forest and jungle. The magnificence of the trees has to be seen to be believed, among them teak, oaks, chestnuts and birches. As it was April there was also a sudden froth of blossom among them, the pink of a carmine cherry or the white flowers of a crab, even huge camellias.[1] As Ethel pointed out, the forest

---

[1] I am indebted to *Plant Hunter in Manipur* by F. Kingdon-Ward for enabling me to identify these as *Prunus cerasoides rubrea*, *Pyrus Pashia* and *Camellia drupifera*.

always appears a mixture of spring and autumn, as some trees are dropping their leaves or keeping them on while others are clothed in the fresh greens of spring. This is because some deciduous trees shed their leaves in the cold weather of December to January, while others, particularly those at a lower altitude, drop theirs in the hotter months of March to April. A very colourful touch is added to the woodlands by the new laurel leaves tipped with fiery crimson, and pieris and acers, whose fresh leaves appear before the last of their old ones drop, so that they are still shot with autumn colours in the spring.

Towards the Imphal plain the landscape of forest and jungle opens out into an idyllic scene: green meadows interspersed with blue rivers, graceful trees and bamboo groves. Lining the road are hedges of wild roses, with tiny pink sprays of flowers, while the blue hills stretch endlessly into the distance. Once on the plain the names of the Manipur villages started to become familiar. We stopped at Sengmai so that one of our veterans could revisit a battle site; it was here that Frank had ridden to greet Quinton, and first heard with dismay about his plan to arrest the Senapati at the durbar.

By now the plain we were travelling through was bathed in golden evening light, so it looked as calm and peaceful as when Ethel had seen it for the first time. It was almost possible to believe the Manipur Tourist Board's proud claim that its people are 'multiple ethno-cultural streams merging into patterns like a gently blended water-colour'. Sadly, politically, Manipur is a very troubled country, undergoing some of the worst turbulence in its long history. One of the reasons is that the population is divided into three main tribes, the traditionally warlike Nagas and Kukis of the hills, and the gentler Meiteis of the plain. These in turn have 29 sub-divisions, not unlike the Scottish clans with their 'septs'. As one member of the Assam Rifles put it, 'every 25 kilometres along the road you come across a new tribe'. Since Manipur voted (reluctantly) to join the Indian Union in 1949, two years after independence, there has been a struggle by the tribes and sub-tribes to form their own independent states along ethnic lines. Each is caught up in insurgency, fighting for its own land and rights, and banditry is rife. Abductions, murders and rapes fill the daily headlines in the papers. Those on the front page of the *Imphal Free Press*[2] on one day of our visit alone read: 'Two of four abducted persons found killed', 'Keirange residents save two from kidnap gangsters' and 'Superintending Engineer State Public Works Dept. Irabot Singh, kidnapped by unknown persons'.

Satya Sagar, writer and journalist, points out in his article 'Manipur: India's Intifada'[3] that 'successive Indian governments since independence have been guilty of treating the north-eastern provinces as mere property with little respect for their people's culture, aspirations and demands ...' 'What makes it worse,' he continues, 'is the reality that these Indian national elites, essentially drawn from upper caste "Aryan" stock, combine the brute technology of the nation-state with the mataphysics of the ancient caste system, thereby asserting a double oppression on all "lesser people" in the land.'[4] He suggests that members of the Indian army and police have Brahminical notions of cultural and racial 'superiority' over those of Tibeto-Burman origin in the north-east.

The Assam Rifles, a locally recruited para-military force, whose officers are seconded from the regular Indian army, have the difficult task of serving as a peace-keeping force in the area following the Armed Forces (Special Powers) Act passed by the Indian government in 1958. Their officers explain that apart from the daily unrest, they fear future danger from China, whose economic boom may create a less fortunate class who will become restless and aggressive. They also fear fundamentalism. It was pointed out that besides its day-to-day tasks, the regiment also involves itself in social work of all kinds, particularly in the educational field.

Despite the good work the Assam Rifles do, their presence is resented because the Armed Forces (Special Powers) Act gives the regiment draconian powers, including the right to arrest and

---

[2] *Imphal Free Press*, 8 April 2006.
[3] 'Manipur: India's Intifada,' Satya Sagar, published on the Internet 30 September 2004.
[4] *Ibid.*

shoot potential troublemakers merely on the strength of a suspicion. Furthermore, their forces can only be prosecuted for their actions with the consent of the Indian government. The anger built up by this means that those serving with the Assam Rifles are vulnerable to accusations of many kinds, including rape and murder. The women of Manipur have always had the reputation of being very strong, and on 15 July 2004 a dozen middle-aged women walked to the gates of the paramilitary headquarters, stripped naked and held up placards reading, 'Indian Army rape us—rape us the way you did Manorama.' Manorama was a Manipuri woman who had been arrested at her house earlier that month for being a suspected insurgent, and was later found dead. Autopsy reports showed that she had been shot through her genitals several times at close range, which the protesters believed had been done to cover up evidence of rape.

Political unrest, influenced by Gandhi's 'non-cooperation' movement, began again in Manipur in 1931, the country having enjoyed forty years of peace following 1891. Agitation increased in 1936 when Manipur found itself among the 17 small states carved out of the Assam States Agency. Hijam Irabot, a Manipuri, became leader of a party calling for more democratic government in the country, a movement from which the Maharajah and the British disassociated themselves. After World War II Irabot returned to Manipur and founded the Praja Sangh party, which opposed unification with India. He was defeated, however, in the election of 1948 by the Manipur State Congress Party, which favoured the merger. Following this, a great many new parties sprang up, including the United National Liberation Front (the biggest militant group, whose mission is to fight the Indian colonial army and antisocial elements), the Manipur People's Army, Into Burma Liberation Front and PREPAK, an underground organisation.

In the early 1990s, hostility was fuelled between the Nagas and Kukis, followed by horrific episodes of 'ethnic cleansing' and the torching of hundreds of houses by the warring tribes. Eventually even the Meiteis, the peaceful plain dwellers, were drawn in. At the time of writing there are said to be 18 or more insurgent organisations in Manipur. These have now turned against each other, and banditry reigns. Manipuris see little hope of economic growth or an end to unemployment while the Armed Forces (Special Powers) Act is in force. There are many calls to repeal it, although this seems unlikely in the present climate.

There is also a cultural revivalist movement, whose main demand is to restore Meitel Mayek, the original Manipuri script which was replaced by Bengali lettering nearly three centuries ago. This led in 2005 to the burning of Manipur's central library, and the destruction of thousands of precious scripts.

Politics apart, Manipur, 'Land of the Jewel', having been cut off from mainstream India for almost all its existence, has, amongst all the countries in the world, probably the greatest number of things that are unique about it—not only its festivals, beliefs and dance, but also a very rare flora and fauna. Only in Manipur can the national flower, the 'Sirhoi' or Manipur lily, be found growing wild. It grows on the Sirhoi range to the north-east of the country, and the delicate pink bell-shaped flowers, which appear between June and July, flourish at a height of 8,000 feet, so are not seen by many.[5] Unique, too, is the Sangai, or 'dancing deer',[6] now, sadly, a critically endangered species, its last existing natural habitat being the Kaibul Lanjao Floating National Park in the Loktak lake. We were impressed by how sensitive the Manipuris appear to be to conservation. They now understand the danger of commercial exploitation of their forests, and display 'anti-plastic' signs in Imphal and elsewhere.

Our first preoccupation on our arrival in Imphal was to locate the old palace, for this would help us find our bearings. It was not easy, as we were strictly confined to our coach. It was only when we passed the terracotta walls of what is now known as 'Kangla' that we realised that they enclosed the original pât of the palace and fort. The area was considerably larger than I had imagined, and partly surrounded by an attractively wide moat (described in the plan in Ethel's book as a wet ditch). The wall, which is

---

[5] *Plant Hunter in Manipur*, F. Kingdon-Ward.
[6] *Cervus Eldii*, also called Eld's or brown-antlered deer.

interspersed with white posts and a guardtower, stands on the palace side of the moat, on a high bank. This, we presumed, was all that was left of the old outer wall, which was already marked as being in ruins in 1891. We drew a breath of excitement as the main gateway, now called the Kangla gate, came into view; it looked identical to the 1891 drawing of it in the *Illustrated London News*. We were not allowed into the gate to see the ruins of the old palace, although from photographs they appear to be very large sandstone pillars. The area, which until recently served as barracks to the Assam Rifles, lies opposite the site of the old Residency, in the grounds of which the Governor now resides. The British officers who were murdered in 1891 lie buried to the left side of the banqueting hall under an Indian style marble monument which reads:

> The Government of India
> have caused this monument to be erected
> to mark the spot where rest the remains of
> THE BRITISH OFFICERS
> who were murdered at Manipur
> 24th March 1891
> —
>
> JAMES WALLACE QUINTON, CSI ICS
> COLONEL CHARLES McDOWAL SKENE DSO ISC
> FRANK St.CLAIR GRIMWOOD ICS
> WILLIAM HENRY COSSINS ICS
> LIEUTENANT WALTER HENRY SIMPSON ISC
> —
>
> IN THE SAME GRAVE ARE DEPOSITED THE REMAINS OF
> LIEUTENANT LIONEL WILHELM BRACKENBURY ISC
> AND OF SEVERAL SOLDIERS OF THE 44TH GURKHA RIFLES
> WHO FELL IN ACTION IN MANIPUR
> ON THE SAME DAY

One advantage of having to drive everywhere in Imphal was that we had a bird's eye view of the ever-entertaining life of the road. Our driver's second string was a young beady-eyed boy whom we nicknamed 'the artful dodger': his main duty (when not handing us in and out of the coach aided by a small stool whose wickerwork was giving way!) appeared to be to hurl invective at any unfortunate rickshaw driver who crossed our path. Fortunately we were able to make two expeditions on foot. The first, on which we were heavily guarded by tanks, was to the moving and superbly kept war cemetery, where the heroes of the 14th army campaign lie enshrined with touching memorials from their family inscribed on their tombs, although several remain unknown.

The famous Women's Market (still going strong) was another permitted five-minute stroll from our hotel. It is still, I believe, an institution unique to the world. Just as when Ethel visited it in 1891, only women are allowed to sell in the market. It is an enchanting sight to see row after row of them, often sitting four or five deep, selling all manner of things: vegetables, dried fish, fruit, spices, and their own speciality of boiled soya bean wrapped in a banana leaf. Some sit behind mounds of brassware, and others behind piles of cloths, clothes and the woven goods for which they are famous. It is said that every household owns a loom. We made our way towards the stalls selling 'phaneks'. These are the long pieces of cloth with a patterned border which form the traditional Manipuri dress, which many of the women still wear. The phanek, worn over a blouse or T-shirt, is wrapped round the body from the chest to the ankles and neatly tucked in at the side. It is traditionally made of blue and white striped cloth, but today the stripes can be purple, brown or green, while the plain phaneks glow in all the colours of the rainbow. As we were the only foreign tourists walking round the market, the women found us curious, but otherwise took little notice of us, although those who did were very ready with their smiles and laughter. Our Manipuri guide, Ayai Shimray, guided us round expertly until we finally flopped in the heat, and found boxes on which to sit and enjoy the colourful scene.

It was through Ayai, a Christian Tongkul Naga, that we learned of an important person in Manipur's history, the Reverend William Pettigrew, on whom she was writing her thesis. William, the son of a ship's engineer, was born in Edinburgh in

1869. William's mother died when he was a baby, and his father moved south, and remarried. William was thus educated at a grammar school in the south, and at the age of twenty-one went to India as a missionary under the auspices of the Arthington Aborigines Mission.[7] A year after his arrival, he joined the American Baptists. William later wrote in the *Baptist Missionary Review* of his shock at reading of the events of 1891:

> January 1891 ... I first set foot on Indian soil, and heard two months later of the terrible massacre of seven British officers in Manipur ... from the day we heard in Eastern Bengal of that massacre ... to the day we were given permission to enter this native state in January 1894 preparation[s] in language study and for the experiences ahead of us were the order of the day.[8]

Once in Manipur, William struggled to achieve the Mission's aim of propagating the gospel among the people, a large proportion of whom were animistic, and of the rest, about 60% were Hindu and 4% Muslim. He found himself frustrated by the government of India, who refused to allow any missionary work among Manipur's Hindu population until the young Maharajah, Churachand, came of age. They gave William the option to leave, or confine himself to converting the head-hunting Tanghul Nagas in Ukrul, far away on the border with Upper Burma in the northeast of the country. Here one of the villages had recently suffered a bloody raid in which 140 heads had been cut off and carried away.

William remained isolated in Ukrul for twenty years, slowly winning the confidence of the tribesmen, who were full of animistic fear and superstition. He built a church and a school, where he insisted that lessons should be in Manipuri rather than Bengali, and wrote a Manipuri grammar in English. In his aim to bring the hill tribes together he encouraged inter-tribal marriage.

Gradually William's work became valued by the then British Political Agent, Colonel Shakespear. He was promoted to be a

---

[7] Arthington, a wealthy member of the Society of Friends, left a fortune for missionary work on his death in 1900, having been a lifetime donor.
[8] *Baptist Missionary Review*, vol. XXXVIII, November 1932, no.11.

school inspector, and amongst his other work, he was asked to report on the conditions in the south-west of the state, where the Lushais were suffering a severe famine. Thanks to the education he had given them, he had several young men whom he could now send out to help.

In 1916 William was given permission to move his mission to Kangpokpi, on the road from Imphal to Kohima, a far more central place. 'In this way,' he wrote, 'the Lord opened up the hills in all directions for the preaching of his word, and the gathering in of many souls to his praise and glory.'[9]

Today the Nagas, almost to a man, are devout American Baptists. As two writers from the Reformed Theological Seminary, Jackson, Massachusetts, put it, 'Manipur owes a lifetime of gratitude to this one-man army.' The Meiteis mostly remain followers of Vaishnavite Hinduism, with a small section following the ancient Meitei religion 'Sanamahi Laining', an amalgamation of Christianity, Buddhism and tribal beliefs. The rest of the hill peoples continue to be largely animist.

It was from temple worship and ancient shaman-led pre-Hindu ancestral rituals that the unique Manipuri dances developed. Dance was also an integral part of the Vaishnavite Hinduism introduced into the country in the eighteenth century. Cultural traditions have therefore been preserved in their purest forms and kept out of reach of the western world. 'Every child in Manipur learns to dance,' wrote Ethel, 'they cease when they marry, but up till then they take great pride in their nautches.' The nautch dancers were often asked to the Residency to entertain visitors, and Tikendrajit claimed in his defence at his trial that the British had been deceitful in asking for them during Quinton's visit, while they were secretly plotting his arrest.

An invitation to the Jawaharlal Nehru Manipur Dance Academy to see a demonstration of their unique styles of dance during our visit therefore gave us great pleasure. Dance in Manipur continues to be devotional in nature, as we saw demonstrated in the classical *Ras Lila*, where the love between Rada and Krishna,

---

[9] *Ibid.*

the Divine Master, is conveyed through the dancers' subtle bodily movements. The women have no eye contact, as they wear helmet-shaped headdresses with veils. Instead they wear spectacular dresses: bell-shaped skirts twinkling with tiny mirrors which are sewn into them are stretched over hoops, and have gauze overskirts like a ballerina.

Excitement was kindled in the audience by the *Pung cholom*, in which a band of men beat cylindrical drums with their hands as they leap about the stage to the rhythm. The drumming starts gently, but becomes urgent and rapid as their movements work up to a frenzied climax.

Sparks really began to fly when the art of *Thang-ta* was demonstrated! This is the unique martial art of Manipur, which requires perfect stance and control of the body and feet; it also relies on correct breathing and other disciplines such as meditation. Dramatically dressed in black, two men fought first with sticks, then with wickedly sharp long curved swords, and finally evil-looking hatchet-shaped dhaos, similar to those with which the English officers had been beheaded. We gasped as they fought. Their dexterity was incredible, and it looked as if at any moment a fatal stroke would end the contest. The climax was breathtaking. One of the swordsmen lay on his back with a melon next to his throat while the other was elaborately blindfolded in front of the audience. To the accompaniment of chants from the prone man, and drums and cymbals, the blindfolded swordsman made rhythmic movements about the room—then suddenly leapt towards the prostrate body in a precise pattern, chopping the air as he went, and with one swift stroke cut the melon in two without drawing a drop of blood! We returned to our hotel feeling decidedly limp!

It was while we were breakfasting on our second morning in our modest hotel that the following invitation from the Maharajah's office was read out:

HEARTIEST WELCOME TO THE ROYAL BRITISH LEGION

THE SANA KONUNG SEMGAT LUP *(the Royal Palace Development Council) warmly and profoundly welcomes the*

31-member Team of the Royal British Legion. Some of them are War Veterans of the World War II, who arrived in Manipur to offer floral tributes to the Cemetery of their deceased and reverential forefathers who sacrificed their valuable lives to protect, defend and uphold the pride and prestige of the British Nation, and further earnestly requests the Team to kindly make it convenient to visit the Sana Konung (New Palace) at Palace Compound, Imphal and meet with His Highness the King of Manipur who expresses his ardent desire to host the team at the Palace.

Who could refuse such an invitation? As the afternoon approached we polished our shoes and got into our tidier clothes before going by coach to the palace which, we learned, had been built for the young boy Rajah Churachand by the British in 1904. The imposing front looked in need of restoration, as did the grounds, but that could be expected. We took off our shoes on the steps before being ushered into a large dark durbar hall, which smelled deliciously of jasmine, little scented joss sticks having been placed around it. There we were hospitably greeted and offered a wrapped rice cake and banana on a plantain leaf by the elderly royal ladies, who fluttered round us like beautiful moths.

As we were given a long introduction to the palace by an elderly chamberlain, our eyes started to distinguish our surroundings, thanks to small stained-glass windows above the doors, and some dim electric lighting which flickered on and off continuously, as it did in our hotel. We could see that the blue-green walls were peeling badly and showing obvious signs of damp, and had portraits of the royal family on them. In front of us stood a dais with a wooden throne on it.

Anticipation built up as we awaited the much-heralded arrival of the 'king', as his courtiers liked to call him. Eventually he walked in: a good-looking, upright young man of 25 dressed in a black Chinese-style suit. He took his place on the throne, looked rather obviously at his watch, then sat still and Buddha-like with a glazed expression as we were subjected to yet another long speech by the Chancellor. The king then conducted a quick shake of hands before addressing us. With an effort we caught the gist of his words: the palace was falling down, so please would we, on our return to England, ask the Queen to give her personal financial help to restore it?

After a long speech by another member of the court, we were given the irresistible invitation to inspect the palace 'upstairs'. Fascinated, we started to climb the imposing staircase whose rails shook unnervingly when held, and whose steps were visibly parting from the wall. We made it to the top only to find that we had reached a ruin! As we picked our way gingerly over the roof we were attended by a bevy of polite courtiers, whom we were able to quiz a little about the king, Leisemba Sanajaoba, and his background. We learned that he was a great-grandson of the boy Rajah Churachand through his father and was already married, with a son and daughter. He lived in the palace—though where exactly, we couldn't fathom! He had not, like his ancestor, had an education out of Manipur, and no longer had any influence on Manipur affairs, the last Maharajah to have done so having been his grandfather, Bodchandra Singh. In 1947 the latter had dissolved the Manipur State Durbar preceding the first democratic elections held the following year, although still without general suffrage. Any remnants of power remaining to the Maharajah vanished at the union with India in 1949.

We later learned that if the Maharajah and state were willing, the palace could have become a World Heritage Site, but that they were reluctant to give up their independence in the matter. Instead, when we were reunited with our shoes, we noticed a collection bowl discreetly placed on the steps.

Polo, so beloved of Frank Grimwood, is still flourishing in Manipur, its birthplace, and we were fortunate to be invited to watch the weekly game of the All Manipur Polo Association, one of whose three patrons is Prince Charles. It was not, alas, being played on the old historic ground inside the old palace pât, as this was being restored. It would have been very emotional to have watched from the lawn where Ethel had once sat admiring the Senapati's dashing play, and where he was eventually hanged. The current ground, however, had a beautiful setting, with lovely views of the surrounding hills. We mixed freely with the few spectators, and I found myself sitting next to a cousin of the Maharajah and adviser to the Polo Association, who was very informative about the game. In Manipur, he explained, polo is played on small mountain ponies that are tough enough not to have to be changed between chukkas, but not high enough to qualify for international games. Their saddles are heavy, with a pair of leather flaps at the sides to protect the legs of the rider. He pointed out to me the special turban or 'koiyet' which the players wear instead of a helmet—a length of cloth elaborately swathed round the head and fastened under the chin. The two opposing teams, seven players in each, wore white or tangerine-coloured tops, and were a magnificent sight as they lined up ceremonially before starting the game. This is started by the ball being thrown in from the centre line. There are no goal posts, but once the ball passes the back line a bell is rung and a goal awarded. It was amusing to see, after the official game was over, the local boys mount the ponies and race them, hell for leather, round the ground—natural riders, all of them.

My neighbour was interested in Manipur's history, and therefore happy to talk about the 'Anglo-Manipuri' war. He explained that the site of Khongjom, the culminating battle, was only about fifteen miles from Imphal, and a visit we should definitely try to make, but alas, we didn't. Manipuris, because of the valour with which their people fought, claim Khongjom as a victory, even though they were defeated, and their independence brought to an end. The stock answer to the *cause* of the war, of which Tikendrajit is viewed as the hero and martyr, is always the same: 'Well, the British interfered in our home affairs.'

We regretted missing Khongjom, and that there were so many other places which remained unvisited in this beautiful country. We should have liked to see the State Museum by the polo ground, and the Loktak Lake, the largest freshwater lake in north-east India, where the Grimwoods used to camp, and shoot wild duck and geese.

My greatest sadness was that we were not able to visit the grave of Frank Grimwood and his fellow officers, for they deserved to have a prayer said over them. However, we were very pleased to hear afterwards from Dr R. K. Nimai Singh, the Governor's Secretary, that the present Governor has had the grave restored, and the whole area replanted with trees and shrubs.

There is much to regret in Manipur, particularly the political disorder. Even so, there is also much to admire: the people's proud independence, ecological awareness, crafts, dancing, festivals and technological skills, and the beautiful countryside.

As our aeroplane rose from Imphal airport and circled towards the surrounding hills we thought of the courtesy we had received on our visit, and prayed that things might improve for Manipur in the future; that the good intentions of all who have loved and served her might one day be rewarded.

Bibliography

Assam District Gazetteer, vol. IX: 'Naga Hills & Manipur'. B. C. Allen, Baptist Mission Press, Calcutta, 1905.
Bence-Jones, Mark. *The Viceroys of India*, Constable & Co, London, 1982.
Bennett, Mary. *The Ilberts in India: An Imperial Miniature*, British Association for Cemeteries in South Asia (BACSA), London, 1995.
Census of India 1891. Assam, Assam Secretariat Printing Office, Shillong, 1892.
Coen, T. Creagh. *The Indian Political Service: A Study in Indirect Rule*, Chatto & Windus, London, 1971.
Couchman, G. H. H. *The Manipur Expedition 1891*, prepared under orders of the Quarter-Master General, India, 1891. Published Simla, 1892.
Creagh, Sir O'Moore & Humphris, E. M. (eds). *The Victoria Cross and D.S.O*, Standard Art Books, London, 1924.
Esher, Lord & Buckle, G. F. (eds). *Letters & Journals of Queen Victoria*, vol. 2, John Murray, London, 1907–1936 (Third series).
Forsyth, Douglas. *Autobiography and reminiscences*, ed. by his daughter, Bath, 2001.
Ghose, Mano Mohun. *Did the Manipur Princes Obtain a Fair Trial?*, William Hutchison & Co., London, 1891.
Gilmour, David. *The Ruling Caste, Imperial Lives in the Victorian Raj*, John Murray, London, 2005.
Grimwood, Ethel. *My Three Years in Manipur and Escape from the Recent Mutiny*, Richard Bentley & Son, London, 1891.
India Office List 1891 (British Library: BL, OIR254.54).
Ingram, Alison. *Index to the Archives of Richard Bentley & Son 1829–1898*, Cambridge, 1977.
Johnstone, Major General Sir James. *My Experiences in Manipur and the Naga Hills*, Sampson Low, Marston and Company Ltd, London, 1896.
Jyotirmoy, Roy. *History of Manipur*, Firma KLM, Calcutta, 1999.
Kingdon-Ward, F. *Plant Hunter in Manipur*, Alden Press, Oxford, 1952.
Lal, Dr. Dena (ed.). *History of Modern Manipur 1826–1949*, Orbit Publishers, New Delhi, 2001.
Mahajan, Sneh. *British Foreign Policy 1874–1914: The Role of India*, Routledge, London, 2002.
Manual of Instructions to Officers of the Political Department of the Government of India, 1924.
McCulloh, M. *Valley of Manipur*, Gian Publications, Delhi, 1980.
Mitra, Surendra Nath. *The Manipur War*, Banerjee Press, Calcutta, 1891.
Morse, Belinda. *John Hanson Walker, The Life and Times of a Victorian Artist*, Alan Sutton, 1987.

Parratt, John. *Queen Empress vs. Tikendrajit, Prince of Manipur*, Har-Anand Publications, New Delhi, *ca.* 1992.
Sagar, Satya. 'Manipur: India's Intifada', published on the Internet, 30 September 2004.
Saha, Ranajit Kumar. *Valley Society of Manipur*, Punthi-Pustak, Calcutta, 1994.
Singh, N. Khelchandra. *Documents on Anglo-Manipur War 1891*, N. Debendra Singh, Imphal, 1984.
Singh, N. Khelchandra. *The Battle of Khongjom*, Imphal, 1984.
Singh, Rajkumar (ed.). *Peeps into Manipur*, Rajkumar Publications, Imphal, Manipur, 1985.
Slim, William Viscount. *Defeat into Victory*, Cassell, London, 1956.
Tarapot, Phanjoubam. *Bleeding Manipur*, Har-Anand Publications PVT Ltd., New Delhi, *ca.* 2003.
Thomas, C. J., Krishnan, R. Gopal and Singh, R. K. Ranjan. *Constraints in Development of Manipur*, Regency Publications, New Delhi, *ca.* 2001.
Turner, Michael L. *Index and Guide to the Lists of the Publications of Richard Bentley & Son*, 1975.

Newspapers and magazines

Baptist Missionary Review, vol. 38, Nov. 1932, no. 11.
Compilation from the *Pioneer* newspaper, Allahabad, 1891.
The Englishman, 4 May 1891.
Illustrated London News, 4, 11, 18, 25 April, 2, 9, 30 May, 6, 13, 27 June, 1, 8 August, 28 November 1891.
Imphal Free Press, 8 April 2006.
The Lady 30 April and 7 May 1891.
The Times, March–November 1891.
Yaquina Bay Times, 16 August 1928.

Index

Albany, Oregon 112
Alexandra, Princess of Wales 83
All Manipur Polo Association
    128–9
American Baptists 124–5
ammunition 34, 50, 52
Andaman Islands 89
Anglo-Manipuri War 57–8, 129
Apcar, Mr 65
Armed Forces (Special Powers) Act
    119, 121
Army, 14th 115–6, 123
Ashland, Oregon 112
Assam 56, 71
Assam District Gazetteer 3
Assam Rifles 115, 118–20, 122
Assam States Agency 120

Baptist Missionary Review 124
Barnett, Charles William 109
Barnett, 'Miss' Emily (Mrs
    Mudstone) 109
Barraud, Herbert 82, 107
Beaufort Street, Chelsea 109
Bengal 88, 104
Bengal Civil Fund 83
Bentley, George, publisher 93, 96,
    101, 103
Birch, Capt. A. 66
Bishenpur 43, 115
Bodchandra Singh, Maharajah 128
Boileau, Capt. 24, 26, 28–30, 39, 40,
    41, 43, 48, 51, 60, 66–70, 75
Boileau, Col. Digby 70

Boisragon, Capt. Alan 15, 65, 109,
    110
Boisragon, Maj. Gen. Theodore 98,
    108–9
Brabazon, Col. John Arthur Henry
    Moore 110
Brackenbury, Lieut. Lionel
    Wilhelm 24, 31, 33–5, 40, 50
Brindaban 17
Brown, Dr, Political Agent,
    Manipur 77
Burma 3, 4, 71, 124
12th Burma Infantry 55
Butcher, Capt. 31, 33, 35, 39, 41, 43,
    51, 67–9, 75–6, 77, 99
Bysak, Babu Janoki Nath 76

Cachar, district of 6, 42–44, 48, 49,
    52, 60, 113
Calcutta 21, 65, 74, 76, 99, 109
Calvert, Surgeon 38–9, 40, 42, 51,
    60, 69
Cambridge, Duke of 98
Carnegy, Capt. 57
Carshalton, Surrey 110
Chandrakirti Singh, Maharajah 5
Chatterton, Lieut. 31, 36–7, 67–8
Chatterton, Richard 111
Child's Companion, The 96
Churachand, Maharajah 89–91,
    124, 127, 128
Clackamas, Oregon 111
Collett, Brig. Gen. 21, 50, 58, 60–1
Connaught, Duke of 98

INDEX

Cossins, William Henry   36, 61–3
Cowley, Capt.   42, 46–8, 66, 69, 100
Cross, Viscount, Minister of State for India   69, 70, 72, 79, 85–6
Cross, Viscountess   80

dance   125–6
Davis, A.W.   74
Defeat into Victory (Slim)   115
dhaos (knives)   44, 62–3, 126
Dilling & Sons, printers   101
Drury, Capt.   57
Durand, Capt.   5
Durand, Sir Mortimer, Secretary to Government of India   77, 98
Durbar, British   10–11, 24–7, 29
Durbar Room, Manipur   61–3

East India Company   84
Eden, Hon. Sir Ashley   104
Englishman, The   99–100
Evans, Col.   66

Flahaut, Comte de   84
Forsyth, Sir Douglas   93

Galbraith, Maj. Gen.   68
Gandhi, Mahatma   120
Gauhati   14
Gerrard, Margaret Emma (see Moore)
Ghose, Mano Mohan   76–7, 86
Government of India   2, 20–1, 50, 66, 69, 71, 78, 83–4, 89–90, 92
Governor-General (see Viceroy)
Graham, General   60, 65
Grant, Lieut. (later Major) Charles, V.C.   18, 20, 54–60
Grimwood, Ethel (née Moore)
  adventure with bear   96
  appearance   80, 97, 104
  arrival in Cachar   65, 98
  arrival in England   65
  arrival in Manipur   8–11
  attack on Residency   33–40
  audience with Queen Victoria   80–1
  ayah   16, 30

Grimwood, Ethel—*cont.*
  change of name   111
  character   81, 94, 100, 102, 113
  clothes   104, 107
  criticisms of   65–6, 77, 98–9, 100
  death   112
  departure for Jorehat   14, 117
  education   88
  emigration   111
  escape from Residency   40–3, 113
  family   1–2, 108–110
  funeral   113
  garden   96–7
  hill bungalow   97
  ill-health   112
  jewellery   107, 113
  journey to Manipur   5–9
  knowledge of terrain   16, 100, 113
  language lessons   13, 96
  letter to Capt. Boileau   39–40
  letters from Queen   85, 86
  letters to Queen   85, 88–9
  letters to Lieut. Williams   21–2
  letter to sister-in-law, Mabel   38–9, 49, 112
  life in Residency   11, 23, 94, 97
  march to Cachar   43–9
  marriage   2, 109, 110
  menagerie   96
  murder of Frank   52–3
  music teacher   111
  My Three Years in Manipur
    publication and profits   93–7, 98, 103
    quotes from   1, 5, 11–12, 15–16, 24, 31, 35–6, 38, 39, 41–2, 43, 47, 48, 52, 94, 96, 99, 100, 101, 103, 113–4, 125
    reviews   101–2
    success of   102–3
  pensions, state and other   83, 113
  portrait   104, 106–7
  praise for   38, 44–5, 52, 99
  relations with husband   32, 38, 52, 98, 100–1

134

INDEX

Grimwood, Ethel—*cont.*
  relations with Senapati 11, 25–6, 80, 81–3, 85, 88–9, 99
  return to England 65
  return to Manipur 16, 18
  Royal Red Cross medal 81, 105, 106
  social life 6, 18, 24
  telegrams to and from 76–7
  visit to Hove 88–93
  visit to Tammu 18, 20
  will 112–3
Grimwood, Frank, Political Agent, Manipur
  abdication of Maharajah Surchandra, 17–18
  arrival in Manipur 8–11
  attack on Residency 33–7
  attempted arrest of Senapati 24–5, 29–31, 118
  burial 61
  character 101
  criticism of 15–6, 65–6, 77, 92
  defence of 102
  departure from Manipur 13–4, 117
  durbar at Residency 10–11, 24–7, 29
  early career 1–2
  education 1
  family 3, 88, 93, 108
  grave and memorial 129
  hill bungalow 97
  journey to Manipur 5–9
  language lessons 13, 96
  letters from 22–3
  life in Residency 11, 97
  marriage 1–2
  memorials 97, 107–8
  menagerie 96
  murder of 61
  nautch dancers 31, 32
  photography 13, 15–6, 18, 77
  political agent, role as 2, 11, 13, 20
  polo playing 4, 11
  relations with Ethel 32, 38, 52

Grimwood, Frank—*cont.*
  return to Manipur 15–6
  truce negotiations 36–7
Grimwood, Jeffrey 88, 93
Grimwood, Mabel 38–9, 49, 85, 98, 112
Grimwood, Major 60
Grimwood, Zoe 88, 93
Gurdon, Lieut. 22–4, 37, 41, 50
Gurkha Rifles
  2–4th 54, 57
  42nd 21–2, 24, 44, 47
  43rd light infantry 21, 42, 47, 64, 69, 87
  44th 24, 74, 94

Heath, Mr, Political Agent, Manipur 13–14, 15–16, 60, 117
hill bungalow 97
Hood, Dr Wharton 85
Hove 88, 93

Ilbert, Sir Courtenay and Lady 74
Illustrated London News 45, 64, 65, 78, 101–2, 106, 107, 122
Imphal 3, 7–9, 50, 55, 60, 61, 66, 72, 115–6, 117
Imphal Free Press 119
India Office, Whitehall 50, 70, 71
Indian Civil Service 1, 73–4, 79, 90, 109
Indian Government 119–20
Indian Mutiny 57
Irabot, Hijam 120

Jhiri river 6, 47
Johnstone, Maj-Gen. Sir James, Political Agent, Manipur 5, 10, 51–2, 60, 75, 83, 89
Jorehat, Assam 14, 117
Jyotirmoy, Roy 87–8

Kaibul Lanjao National Park 121
Khongjom, battle of 57–8, 129
King's Royal Rifles 61

INDEX

Kohima 18, 22, 29, 50, 58, 60, 74, 115–7
Kukis 30, 118, 120
Kulachandra (Maharajah/Regent) 16–18, 19, 20, 22–3, 25–7, 29–30, 51, 52, 54–6, 58, 63, 72, 78, 89

Lady, The 107
Lahkipur 48
Lambe, William 109
Langthabal Fort 16, 50, 94
Lansdowne, Henry 5th Marquis, Viceroy 2, 51, 57, 70, 72–3, 75, 83–7
Leighton, Frederic, later Lord 104
Leimatak 42, 44, 100
Lincoln's Inn 1
Logtak (Loktak) lake, the 3, 121, 129
Lugard, Lieut. 31, 33, 38, 44–5, 51

McCabe, Mr 71
McNeill, Miss Ina, lady-in-waiting 85
Manipur
 advance on 60
 All Manipur Polo Association 128–9
 American Baptists 124–5
 Anglo-Manipuri War 57–8, 129
 appointment of Churachand Singh 89–90
 Armed Forces (Special Powers) Act 119–20
 attack on Residency 33–41
 British connection with 2
 ceasefire negotiations 86–7
 character of men 4–5
 character of women 4–5, 120
 dance 125–6
 description of country 1–4, 5, 8, 15
 dhaos 44, 62–3, 126
 durbar room 61–2
 ethnic origin of people 4
 feudal system (lalup) 90

Manipur—*cont.*
 geographical position 3
 history of 2–5
 Imphal Free Press 119
 Irabot, Hijam 120
 Jawaharlal Nehru Dance Academy 125–6
 'Jewel of India' 2, 121
 Kaibul Lanjao National Park 121
 Kangla 121
 Khongjom, battle of 57–8, 129
 King, the 128
 Lily, Manipur 120–1
 Logtak lake 3, 129
 Manorama, Thangiam 120
 Mao Thana 116–7
 Meitel Mayak script 121
 monument to murdered British officers 60, 129–30
 murder of officers 60–3
 music 94
 nautch dancers 31, 32, 77, 125
 palace 60, 62, 121–2
  coup 17
  visit to 127–8
 phanek 123
 political parties 120–1
 political situation 118–21
 polo 4, 11–13, 128–9
 polo ponies 4, 12, 128–9
 recapture of Imphal 60
 religions 124–5
 restricted area 115–6
 Royal family 8, 9, 13, 16
 Royal palace 126–8
 sangai deer 121
 Satya Sagar article 119
 scenery 117–8
 State archives 87–8
 strategic importance 3, 71
 tourist board 118
 trial of the princes 74–9
 tribes 4, 118–20, 123–5
 union with India 128
 unique features 121
 war cemetery 123
 weather 97

136

INDEX

Manipur—*cont.*
  women's bazaar 28–30, 123
  World War I 90
  World War II 115–6
Mao Thana 116–7
Margaret Street, London 109
Mayo College, Ajmer 90
Maxwell, Major St.John, Political Agent, Manipur 71, 72, 74
Meath, Earl of 2
Meiteis 118, 120
Melville, Percy 20, 29, 50
Merton College, Oxford 1, 107–8
Michell, Lt. Col. St. John 60, 65, 74, 76, 98–9
Military Court of Enquiry 66–70, 83
Mill House Paper Mill, Carshalton 110–11
Miller, Andrew Cornwall 110–11, 113
Miller, Evelyn (Ethel) 111–12
Moeser, Mrs 106
Moore, Beatrice (Mrs Ainslie) 88, 110, 113
Moore, Charles William (Ethel's father) 108–10
Moore, Charles William (Mudstone, later Moore) 109–10
Moore, Elizabeth 109
Moore, John, coachmaker 109
Moore, Lilian (Mrs W.B.Maxwell) 88, 109, 112
Moore, Major Martin James 109–10
Moore, Margaret Emma (Ethel's mother) 98, 108–9
Moore, Susannah 110
Moore, Sydney 88, 109–10
Moore, William 52
Moulson, Mrs 88
Mudstone, Charles 109
My Experiences in Manipur (*see* Johnstone, Maj.Gen)
My Three Years in Manipur (*see* Grimwood, Ethel)
Mynzarrow, Mya 71

Nagas 6–7, 30, 34, 44, 97, 116, 118, 120, 123, 124, 125
National Archives, London 98
National Portrait Gallery, Washington D.C. 106
nautch dancers 31, 32, 77, 125
New York 1
Newport, Oregon 111, 112
Nightingale, Florence 81
North East Frontier clasp 70

Oregon, USA 112–14
Oriental Club, Hanover Square 109

Palace, King's 121–2
Pettigrew, Rev. William 123–5
Phipps, Hon. Harriet, lady-in-waiting 88
Pioneer, The 60–1, 76
Political Agents, role of 2–3, 11, 13, 20, 90
polo 4, 12, 128–9
Portland, Oregon 111–12
Presgrave, Capt. 55–6, 60
Primrose, Mr, Political Agent, Manipur 77
Princely (Native) States 2

Quinton, James Wallace, Chief Commissioner of Assam 18, 20–6, 28–9, 31, 33–4, 36–7, 50, 53, 61–3, 66, 74, 118
Quinton, Mrs 83

Regent, the (*see* Kulachandra Singh, Maharajah)
religions of Manipur (see Manipur)
Rennick, Col 60, 71
Residency, British 10, 26, 33–7, 43, 60
Ridgeway, Major Richard V.C. 74
Ripon, Marquis of 66
Roberts, Gen. Sir Frederick, C-in-C India 57, 83
Royal Academy, London 104–5
Royal British Legion 115–6, 127

INDEX

Royal Red Cross medal 81, 99, 104–7
Rundall, Capt. 57–8

St.George's, Hanover Square 110
St. Peter's, Cranley Gardens 2
Sagar, Satya 119
Salisbury, Lord, Prime Minister 86
Sanajaoba, Leisemba, Maharajah 128
Sanatombi, Princess 71
Senapati, Tikendrajit Singh (Jubraj)
   appearance of 9, 11–13, 78
   attack on his palace 34, 75
   attempted arrest of 22–7, 29–31, 75, 102, 118
   capture of 72
   character 11–12, 23, 51, 129
   coup against Maharajah Surchandra 17, 65, 92
   disputes with Royal family 16–7
   dress 12
   efforts to save 86–7
   execution of 87–8, 89
   nickname 23
   polo and other sports 12–13
   public duties 24
   relationship with Ethel 11, 43, 80, 85, 88–9
   role in murder of officers 36, 54, 56, 61–3, 90
   sentence 79, 86, 89
   strength 23
   trial of 74–7, 125
Sengmai 22–3, 118
Shakespear, Col., Political Agent, Manipur 124
Shillong 15, 20, 52
Shimray, Ayai 123
Silchar 6
Simla 51, 76
Simpson, Lieut. Walter Henry 16, 20, 24, 29–30, 36, 61–4
Singh, Angao Sena (later Senapati) 18, 89
Singh, Bhairabijit (Pucca Sena) 77
Singh, Bodchandra, Maharajah 128
Singh, Chandrakirti, Maharajah 5
Singh, Churachand, Maharajah 89–91, 124, 127, 128
Singh, Kulachandra, Maharajah/Regent 16–20, 22–3, 25–7, 29–30, 51–2, 54–6, 58, 63, 72, 78, 89
Singh, Nimai, Dr.R.K 130
Singh, Samoo 8
Singh, Surchandra, Maharajah 11, 16–8, 20
Singh, Tikandrajit Bir, 'Koireng' (see Senapati)
Singh, Zillah 16, 89
Skene, Col. Charles McDowal 21, 25, 28, 30, 31, 34, 36, 61–3, 75, 83
Slim, General 115
Stewart, Robert 106–7
Surchandra, Maharajah 11, 16–17, 20
Surma River 6
Sylhet, W.Assam 2, 5, 89

Tammu, Burma 18, 50, 55–6, 59
Tauchnitz of Leipzig, publishers 101
Thangal General, the 14, 16, 24, 61–3, 72, 75–6, 78, 79, 81, 86–8, 89, 117
Thapa, Naik Kabinaj 74
Thobal 55
Tikendrajit Bir Singh (see Senapati)
Times, The 50, 51, 77, 90, 92, 101–2, 104
Travers, Major Eaton 66
trial of the Princes 74–9
Trotter, Major, Political Agent, Manipur 77

Ukrul 124

Vancouver, Canada 113
Vandyk, photographer 95, 107
Viceroy (Governor-General) (see also Lansdowne) 84
Victoria Cross, the 56–7, 105, 106
Victoria, H.M. Queen
   audience with and interest in Ethel 80–1

138

INDEX

Victoria, H.M. Queen—*cont.*
  Ghose's appeal to   86–7
  Journal   80–1, 89
  Indian servants   72
  involvement with India   72
  judgment on punishments   72–4, 79, 85, 87
  letters to   83–4, 85, 86
  letters from   85, 86
  Royal Red Cross   81
  telegrams   72–3, 85–6, 87

Walker, John Hanson   104–5, 106

war cemeteries   115
war veterans   115–16
Williams, Lieut.   21, 22, 69
Wilson, Floyd   112–13
Winchester College   1, 51, 107–8
Windsor Castle   80–1, 85
women's bazaar   28–30, 123
Woods, Lieut.   33, 51
Wykehamist, The   107

Yaquina Bay Times   113

Zillah Singh   16, 89